In Search Of Mr. Right

In Search Of Mr. Right

A 7 Session Study Guide to Help Women Take Charge of Their Lives

Bernard H. Hamilton, Th.M.

Writers Club Press
San Jose New York Lincoln Shanghai

In Search Of Mr. Right
A 7 Session Study Guide to Help Women Take Charge of Their Lives

Writers Club Press
an imprint of iUniverse, Inc.

For information address:
iUniverse, Inc.
5220 S. 16th St., Suite 200
Lincoln, NE 68512
www.iuniverse.com

Contains spiritual references in building a strong spiritual foundation.

ISBN: 0-595-22849-6

Printed in the United States of America

Contents

PREFACE

The question I receive more than any other on a consistent basis comes from single women already considering, already hurt, or already involved with the wrong man. He's generally someone who has the appearance of being emotionally, financially, and spiritually stable. He is also someone who appears to be quite romantic, considerate, and complimentary, with a good sense of humor. These women ultimately discover that Mr. Right is really Mr. Wrong, complete with heavy debt, a low paying job or no job, no plans for the future, and no sense of purpose for even existing, except to exist to use as many women as he possibly can. He also can be mentally cruel to his women.

On the other hand, Mr. Wrong can be quite successful complete with an impressive financial portfolio, an assortment of expensive clothes stocked in his lavishly styled home that houses his custom made luxury automobile. Of course, women do eventually find that this man can't be trusted and he won't make lasting commitments to a relationship because he's too much in love with himself. Which leads to the question I receive more than any other from single women: Where do I find Mr. Right and how will I know that it's him?

Over the next few chapters, I will answer this question from a biblical perspective, hopefully not in a preachy way. Of course, in the end, you'll be the judge of that.

I must preface this booklet by saying that I am not a psychologist or psychiatrist. I'm a pastor of a church with years of biblical counseling experience that has helped save countless of marriages as well as prevent marriages from occurring. My desire is not to preach to you, but to help every female who's been fooled by Mr. Wrong find Mr. Right, and to help her know when she's found him. So if you're frustrated with consistently ending up with the wrong man, let's take a journey down a road designed to help you break your drought in your search for Mr. Right.

1

A LOOK INTO YOUR PAST

During pre-marital counseling, I ask a series of questions to see what kind of home each person came from: Did both parents raise you? Were you close to your mother? Were you close to your father? Did your mother and father fight a lot? Did your mother stay home? Did your mother work outside the home? Did your father have a drinking problem? Was your father a womanizer? Did your father beat your mother? Did you eat meals together as a family? Did you have a happy childhood? Were you even raised by your parents?

A person's home life, or lack there of, sets the tone for the rest of the pre-marriage sessions. When I ask the woman, "What do you expect from a husband?" Many times, the woman's answer will subconsciously resemble what she saw in her father. If he was a godly man, she expects her husband to be morally sound. If her father was a womanizer, she's subconsciously attracted to fun loving adventurous kind of men who have a problem with commitment. If her father was hard-working man who worked all day and all night, she generally is attracted to a man who work all day long even if it includes working two or three jobs at a time. If a woman is raised in chaos, subconsciously she seeks or creates chaos in her relationships. The point that I'm making is that before a woman can find Mr. Right, she must first deal with her own issues that she brings into a relationship. Unresolved issues lead to baggage just waiting to ooze out into the next relationship.

Things to remember: Whoever Mr. Right turns out to be; he was never created to complete a woman, only to love her as "Christ loved

1

the church." Okay, I said something preachy, but it was to make a powerful point. Christ loved the church so much that He died for her. Mr. Right will be a man, if push comes to shove, who will love his woman so much that He will die for her. Mr. Wrong is too busy worrying about himself to lay down his life for anyone else, let alone his woman or his wife. Therefore, get rid of your baggage by examining it and disposing it.

You're background must be completely examined so that you do not subconsciously pursue a man that reminds you of an ungodly, self serving, inconsiderate, uncaring father who failed at being Mr. Right to your mother and her children. As Nancy Reagan use to say, "Just Say No!" That kind of man is a drug you don't need to take.

I will now present to you various women in varying situations. Do anyone of them resemble you? Lets take a look.

The Woman Considering Marriage

The young lady is fresh out of high school with a little baby to raise. She's considering marrying the father of her baby who's a good looking soft-spoken male who still lives at home with his mother. I ask the first question: "So do you love him?" "Yes I do," she replies. "How does he plan on supporting you and the baby?" I ask. "He has a job working at a garage changing tires," she responds. Of course, I don't want to put the young man down. At least he's trying to get his life together, or so it seems. From time to time I even saw him in the congregation on Sunday holding his little baby girl. I continue my questioning. "How much money does he bring home on a monthly basis?" She hesitates, "Hmm, about $450 a month." I ask, "So how much will your monthly rent come to?" She hesitates again, "Hmm, about $550.00 a month, but I'll be working a part-time job on the side to help him out." In my mind, I was pulling for them, but deep down inside I knew that if they married, this relationship was doomed even before it got started.

I continued my questioning, "So who's going to pay for the telephone, water, electric, clothes, insurance, and food bills?" A blank stare came over her face. Frustrated with my questioning, she responded, "I don't know, but we'll get the money from somewhere." Given their situation, they were so in lust with each other, they couldn't see the flaming red flags of disaster slapping them in the face. I suggested that they first think about getting their emotional, financial, and spiritual situations in order before embarking on their quest for marriage. She wouldn't listen. I would find out later by a reliable source that in the young mans pursuit of raising money to take care of his baby and girlfriend, he turned to selling drugs. What a pity. Finally, the young lady had had enough and terminated the relationship as she sought to first get her own life in order before trying to pursue a relationship with a man who had no clue of how to take care of a family, let alone himself. He had been raised with no male role models. The young woman currently has her own place raising their daughter by herself attending church on a weekly basis and growing stronger in her faith day by day. Learning from your mistakes will do that to you. If your mistakes don't kill you, they can be used to make you stronger. What about the man who worked at the garage? As of this writing, he's still living at home with his mother trying to get his life in order.

This young ladies father could never be counted on when she was growing up. Unbeknownst to her, she ended up with men she could never count on when she grew up, because that was what she was used to when she was growing up. That all changed when she discovered that she was far better than an unreliable man. She finally realized that "she was fearfully and wonderfully man" with her completion coming through her relationship with God, not a man. You see, when she discovered who she was emotionally and spiritually, she could spot Mr. Wrong a mile away, and made the conscious decision to stay away from that kind of man from that moment on. And you can to. I know what you're thinking; "Well did she find Mr. Right?" Not yet, but she knows what Mr. Right looks like. Do you?

Session One

1. I have problems finding the right man because......(fill in the blank).

2. When you look into your past relationship, what inconsistencies do you see?

3. Why couldn't the woman considering marriage, on page 3, not see that the man was not right for her at that time?

4. What's a good indication that a man may not have a clue of how to be a good husband, father, or provider when you're considering a mate?

5. When you were growing up, what ways could you count on your father?

6. In what ways have your boyfriends reminded you of your father?

7. My experience has been that all men are......(fill in the blank).

8. Why do some women feel incomplete without a man?

9. How was the young lady fresh out of high school able to overcome her weakness for immature, irresponsible young men?

10. How can you avoid the same pitfall of this young lady?

Things to remember:

1. Your past doesn't have to be you future

2. Think before you leap into a relationship

3. Stop making the same mistakes with the same kind of men.

4. Get your life in order before considering a serious relationship

5. No man can make your life better if you're not better.

6. Make God your number one relationship.

Say to yourself, "God will be number one in my life."

Notes

Write out your personal and professional short-term goals over the next year.

Personal:

    Spiritual—

    Family—

    Psychological—

    Financial—

    Physical—

Professional:

    Career—

    Education—

    Retirement Plans—

Start putting your life in order

Notes

Write out your personal and professional long-term goals over the next five years

Personal:

    Spiritual—

    Family—

    Psychological—

    Financial—

    Physical—

Professional:

    Career—

    Education—

    Retirement Plans—

Start putting your life in order

Other Notes

Start putting your life in order

2

A LOOK AT WHY YOU FAIL

Our society tells a woman each day she's single or she's alone and that she needs a man to complete her. That same woman hears those confirming if not condemning words from her parents, grandparents, aunts, uncles, sisters, and brothers. Did I leave anyone out? Oh yes, the co-workers and the people you run into even in chat rooms. Parents make comments like, "So when are you going to give us some grandkids?" Other relatives make comments like, "You're not married yet? What are you waiting on?" The smooth talking players make comments like, "As fine as you are, no ones swept you off your pretty feet yet?"

The pressure that a single woman has to deal with from so many angles and from so many different directions, that pressure is compounded each time one of her friends gets married and she has to obligate herself to be a bridesmaid in her friends wedding. And then humiliated each time she's asked to try and catch the brides bouquet, as if those little flowers will bring her some kind of magical luck causing the single men to jump out of the woodwork.

This kind of pressure leads thousands of women to settle for less in a man just to say to her parents, relatives, and friends that I have a husband. He's not good for much, but I have one, so stay off my back! With this kind of pressure, a woman routinely fails to check off her list of what she's looking for in a man. Ask yourself this question: "If you are a spiritual minded woman, why are you settling for an unspiritual minded man? "How can a Christian woman be a partner with one man who doesn't believe or live by the biblical mandates that she lives by"(2

Corinthians 6:14)? How can a spiritually minded woman find happiness with a man who's spiritually in the dark? The answer is she can't. This type of relationship leads to much frustration, anger, bitterness, and hostility. A man with no spiritual connection is a dangerous man to consider for a life-long relationship. What I'm saying is that far too many women are looking at the tangibles that men have to offer without exploring the intangible spiritual side of men resulting in much unnecessary heartache and heartbreak. You don't have to go there girlfriend! Stop abusing yourself to appease society! Get in touch with God and let Mr. Right find you. Because whether you know it or not, you're "worth far more than rubies (Proverbs 31:10). But I'm getting ahead of myself and there I go again getting a little preachy. Let me get up off my soapbox and tell you about a female who finally got herself together.

She Overcame The Failure

She didn't think she was pretty enough to keep her man. She was a little overweight but by know means ugly. He was physically fit, well liked, and an All-American kind of guy. He was someone any woman would want to bring home to Mom and Dad. So she tried to stay close enough to him so that know other woman would snatch him. Whatever he wanted from her, she supplied in an effort to keep him calling and interested in her as his possible woman for life. She waited and waited and waited and waited. For three years she waited and still know proposal for marriage, know engagement rings, and no sign from him that he would pop the question.

In a desperate attempt on her part to nudge him in the right direction, she began asking him direct questions regarding marriage. She would say things like, "Don't you love me?" "Haven't I been good to you?" "Why do you treat me this way?" "I thought we had something special?" "Don't you think we'd make a nice married couple?" If you've asks these questions in the past, don't feel bad. Pressure from society does that to a girl every now and then. Well he felt pressured from her and began creating arguments so he could possibly back out of what he considered was a good thing gone bad. He didn't want to marry her because the message she sent to him was, "I need you to complete me." "Without you, I'm an empty shell." "Rescue me from my life of obscurity." I know. It's enough to make you want to throw up. Most importantly, he really didn't find her desirable enough to marry her. He finally broke up with her leaving her devastated and distraught until she examined herself.

When she started seeing herself in a different light, people started seeing her in a different light. Always remember ladies, "You are fearfully and wonderfully made" and "far more precious than rubies." You don't ever need a man to complete you, only to love you. Your completeness can only be found in God and in the way you feel about yourself. You don't ever need a man to validate your self-worth. And since I'm a preacher of the Gospel, I'll throw in this statement. Your completeness can only be found in Christ. Any other avenue for completeness will leave you empty and unfulfilled in the long run.

Within two months of the breakup, this woman joined a fitness center, got involved with various fellowship groups, joined a women's Bible study, and began believing that she was a beautiful woman. By the third month, the old boyfriend was trying to put an engagement ring on her finger telling her how beautiful she looked and how much he missed her. Her response to all his attention: "Thanks but no thanks." A year later, Mr. Right came along and swept her off her feet. That was six years ago and she's still happily married. The old boyfriend is still single and ego-tripping over himself as a single man.

Begin to look at the inner man more than the outer man while cleaning up and examining the inner you. And always remember, a man was never created to complete you, only to love you. Mr. Right understands that principle.

Session Two

1. I don't need a man to complete me because......(fill in the blank)

2. At your age, do you feel pressure to settle down with a man to satisfy the wishes of your parents, grandparents, or any other relative or friend? If so, why or why not?

3. Have you ever settled for less in a man just to say you have somebody? Why or why not?

4. According to the Bible, "How can a Christian woman be a partner with a man who doesn't believe or live by the biblical mandates that she does?" (2 Corinthians 6:14)

   a. Can she truly be happy in such a relationship?
   b. Why would she settle for such a relationship?
   c. What will her reality generally be in such a relationship?

5. According the Chapter Two, a spiritually unequal relationship between a woman and a man leads to what emotional reactions?

6. What biblical qualities are you looking for in man?

7. What are you doing with yourself to attract such a man?

8. Why would such a man be interested in you at this time in your life?

9. How did the woman in chapter two overcome her sense of low self-worth?

10. What must you do to believe that you're just as beautiful as God says you are?

Fill in the blank......"I am beautiful because_____
_____."

Things to remember:

1. With God in your life, your are complete without a man.

2. No matter what someone has told you, you are beautiful in the sight of God.

3. Don't settle for just any guy. Rather, settle on a spiritually sound one.

4. Make sure you're spiritually compatible with the man of your dreams.

5. Strive to make yourself beautiful on the inside as well as the outside.

6. Never settle for a loser.

Say to yourself, "I am a beautiful woman and I deserve the best in a man that God has to offer, both inside and out."

Notes

Write why you will not fail in your pursuit of becoming a better person.

Work at being the best you, you can be

Other Notes

Work at being the best you, you can be

3

WHY SO MANY WOMEN FALL FOR MR. WRONG

L ets get one thing straight. Mr. Wrong can be a very caring person, very loving, and very understanding. What he doesn't possess is the sacrificial love to give his woman the affection, affirmation, and appreciation that she needs on a consistent basis. He has a tendency to be self-centered caring more about himself and his own needs more than those of his partner, though a good Mr. Wrong knows how to pacify his woman by whispering sweet nothings in her ear, buying her various trinkets, and knowing how to strum a woman like a violin player. So why do so many women fall for Mr. Wrong? Let us take a look at this very complicated question.

The Self-Worth Issue

Some women have never heard, "I love you" from their biological fathers. They've never felt like they measure up to the expectations of dear old Dad. Even if Dad was at home, that one absentee statement in their lives has left them with an empty unsatisfied void to contend with. Some women have tried everything they can think of to pry those words from their father's mouth by trying to make him proud of them through working hard at academics, athletics, a successful career, or by being the best little daughter they can possibly be. Some women wait all their lives to hear "I love you" from Dad, but to no avail. The emotional toll can lead a woman down a path of multiple broken relationships, one night stands based on nothing less than sex and a good time.

17

The convenience of the internet has lured thousands of women both married and unmarried into a world of cyber sex, phone sex, and real sex causing many women to gladly escape they're uneventful reality of the here and now. It has also led a number of women down a road of unrealistic romantic fantasies played out only in their mind and imagination causing them not to be able to soberly differentiate between realistic and unrealistic relationships between a man and a woman. This type of unrealistic thinking about a relationship leads women into the arms of men who know how to create an unrealistic fantasy for the purpose of getting from the woman those things he so chooses to get. By the time Mr. Wrong is through spinning his web, the woman is generally too emotionally entangled to gracefully pull herself out. And by that time, most women don't want out any way. He sedates her emotional pain with what appears to be love, affection, and appreciation, but only for the purpose of using her for his own personal pleasures. Mr. Wrong generally seals the deal by seducing the woman into bed for nights of lust and sex telling the woman over and over again how incredibly beautiful and sexy she is. By this point, the woman is completely hooked on the man, blinded by the short-term lust that in most cases will come to an end once Mr. Wrong becomes bored with the relationship ready to move on to his next conquest. Of course, he will give the woman a lame excuse as to why he needs space from the relationship. He'll say something like, "It's not you. It's me." "I just need some space to think everything through." "Everything is happening so fast." For those ladies who have heard these lines, you know the rest of story, and how it ultimately ends. You're usually crushed emotionally. He generally moves on to his next conquest.

Case And Point

Let me share with you a scenario that happens everyday of the week to nice but naive women who happen to be lonely craving a relationship that will ultimately lead to marriage.

1. A man with a good sense of humor who seems to really find you attractive and some one you consider marriage material walks into your life.

2. He appears to be a really nice person because of his external qualities.

    A. He smells good.
    B. He dresses good.
    C. He has the appearance of being a hard worker.
    D. He looks like he has the potential of having financial stability.
    E. His voice sounds really sexy to you.
    F. He doesn't have a ring on his finger.
    G. He treats you like you're the only woman in the room.

3. A friendly relationship builds through a flood of seductive glances and flirtatious conversation.

    A. You both begin to talk about personal aspects of your life.

        1. Where you were raised.
        2. Who raised you.
        3. How you were raised.
        4. How hard or how easy your life has been.
        5. What you're looking for in a relationship
        6. How many serious relationships you've been in.
        7. Things you like to do in an intimate relationship.

4. Flirtatious conversation graduates to friendly lunches or dinners together.

5. Friendly lunches escalate to intimate rendezvous' to each others homes or a nearby hotel.

6. After the intimate aspect of this relationship has been consummated, the real truth about Mr. Wrong begins to surface.

She Finds Out After The Fact That Mr. Wrong Is Actually Married

She's a receptionist sitting at the front desk greeting each visitor that comes into the office. He walks in confident, tall, dark, and handsome. Nicely dressed, charisma is radiating from his nicely toned body. He approaches her desk with the statement, "Hello pretty lady." "I have an appointment with Mr. May." He doesn't know it, but she's already fantasizing about him in her mind. She watches him as he walks by her desk toward Mr. May's office. She lusts in her heart and mind, "Mmmm, nice butt!" as she fantasizes about the possibilities of being with this hot stud of a man. The thought of this man remains in her mind as he finishes his meeting with Mr. May leaving the office to another sales appointment.

The following week, to her surprise, the same man again comes to meet with Mr. May but only this time she greets him with a seductive "hello." He picks up on the tone of her voice and the flirtatious look in her eyes. He replies with a seductive "well hello to you to." At this point, he is flattered that such an attractive female is attracted to him. As he waits in the outer office for his meeting, he stands over her desk humoring her with small talk and playful compliments that leave her as giddy as a schoolgirl. The romantic and sexual tension fills the room. He moves on to his meeting and then on to his next appointment. She is left not able to get him out of her mind. Unknown to him, she thinks about him all the time. She even dreams about him in very erotic ways.

Two weeks later, he again walks into the office to meet with another person in her office. He greets her with a low whispery, "Hello Beautiful," gazing intently into her eyes. She sits mesmerized by his presence, flushed and weak at the knees. She responds with a smile and a "Hi." He knows that she's hers to have if he wants her. As she gets up from behind her desk to run an errand, He responds by saying, "You have some very sexy legs, Mmmm." It is only a matter of time before this sexually charged interaction plays itself out. She replies with a "thank you." He again leaves for his next appointment leaving her hot and bothered lusting about him the rest of the day and night.

The next week he comes in ready to begin closing the deal of intimacy with this lovely woman who craves every minute of his attention. He knows that there is an attraction between them. He knows that she's interested in something more. At the conclusion of their usual small talk conversation, he does something different before going into his meeting. He makes the suggestion of getting together with her for lunch leaving her his business card. She responds with an "OK." "When?" Catching him a little off guard by her quick response, he responds, "I'll call you with the details this afternoon."

These details are the beginning of a series of lunch dates and intimate dinners that conclude in her bedroom or his hotel room finding them embraced in hot sexual intimacy. In the midst of all the romance and sexual activity, she fails to ask one important question assuming that he wasn't. She had been blinded by all the lust and apparent romance. "Assume what?" you ask. You're about to find out. After a three-month whirlwind courtship, he eventually tells her the news that devastates her world for years to come. One evening as they hold each other tight, he tells her, "Baby, I hate to tell you this, but I'm married." He waits until she is hopelessly hooked on him to tell her the truth. She is left confused and emotionally dazed seeing that she thought she had found the man whom she would spend the rest of her life with. She had found Mr. Wrong and Mr. Wrong had found her.

Mr. Wrong then puts damage control in effect by demonizing his wife by telling his lover he doesn't know how long he will stay with his mean wife, but he wants his lover to know that he loves her and that he will work out a way that they can be together. He just wants her to be patient while he works out all the details of his divorce. Even though her mind tells her to get out of the relationship, her heart betrays her by telling her to stay. The divorce never takes place. The final outcome is that the man never leaves his wife. The other woman hangs in the relationship for years holding out hopes that one day she will have him all to herself. That day never comes. He leaves her emotionally shipwrecked, distraught, and angry with all men for a time or for a lifetime. Now to her, all men are dogs never to be trusted again.

Of course you should know that this scenario really does come from a true story. It's played out everyday of the week. Women allow themselves to be victimized because they fail to ask Mr. Wrong the right questions leading to the guarding of their hearts. Anyway, back to the story. From this broken relationship, this emotionally abused woman went through a series of broken relationships and one night stands as she sought so desperately to find someone who would love her for her and no one else. She tried to soothe her pain with empty sexual conquests to prove to herself that she was in fact truly beautiful. It wasn't until she looked within herself and began to take stock of her own life that she was able to find the man she had been looking for all her life. But it didn't happen overnight. Mr. Right wasn't the type of man that she was use to but he was the type of man that she would grow to love immeasurably as she learned to love herself before anyone else and then opened herself up to let him love her as well. Her Mr. Wrong is still with his wife still victimizing any attractive woman on the side who hasn't yet learned to love herself unconditionally.

So many women fall for Mr. Wrong because they don't know what Mr. Right looks like.

Why does that happen? Let's find out in chapter four.

Session Three

1. *Why is the "Player" so good at manipulating a woman into bed and into relationships?*

2. *Why don't more women resist such a smooth operator?*

3. *I'm a sucker for a___(fill in the blank)__kind of guy.*

4. *How could the woman in chapter 3 avoid her misstep with the married man?*

5. *How can a spiritually minded woman avoid being the prey of Mr. Wrong and his sweet bag of tricks?*

6. *What kind of relationship do you have with your father? Has it always been that way?*

7. *How has your relationship with your father helped you or hurt you in your dealings with other men?*

8. *What advise would you give the woman in chapter 3, and have you ever been the woman in chapter 3?*

9. *Have you ever asked yourself, why you fall for the men you do?*

10. *According to chapter 3, what must you do to correct your judgment in selecting a good man?*

Fill in the blank, "I can turn my love life around by _____.

Things to remember:

1. Smooth operators are rough on the inside. Stay away from them.

2. Learn to be a sucker for the Lord.

3. Stay away from married men! You're only setting yourself up for pain.

4. Learn to respect yourself, and don't let anyone disrespect you.

5. Even if your father is a jerk, you don't have to end up with one.

6. Rid yourself of your issues, then love yourself from a biblical perspective.

Say to yourself, "By the grace of God, I will begin to take stock of my own life and look within myself, from a biblical perspective."

Notes

Write why you will see right through the deceitful ploys of Mr. Wrong and why you will never fall for a loser like Mr. Wrong again.

Be smart enough to know better

Other Notes

Be smart enough to know better

4

IN PURSUIT OF FATHER DEAREST

So many women fall for Mr. Wrong because they've lived with Mr. Wrong all their lives. He can be your father, your stepfather, your grandfather, your foster care father, your uncle, your cousins, your mother's boyfriend or many boyfriends. The list can go on and on. He's typically a man who disrespects women in a myriad of ways. He tells her things like "you stupid idiot!" "You don't know what you're talking about." "Shut up you ignorant cow." "Know one wants you." "Get up and get it yourself." "You ugly bat." "You make me sick!" "It makes me sick just to look at you!" And that's just the verbal abuse that women take.

Some young girls are raised in an environment where they see their mothers physically beaten on a regular basis and grow up to think that beatings at the hand of the man of the house is a normal occurrence. No it isn't! No man ever has the right to beat you for any reason.

Some girls are sexual abused causing them to grow up confused about what is and what isn't normal sexual behavior. These women have a tendency to grow up subconsciously drawn to dangerous men who disrespect women because those type of men were a normal part of their lives. "Normal" men who respect women are not seen as normal in the eyes of women raised around and with men who disrespect women. To that woman, a "normal" man is seen as abnormal. He doesn't seem real to her because he wasn't real in her world growing up. Therefore, this type of woman initially is attracted to men she can relate to from her environment. The man who cheats on her or talks down to her or emotionally mistreats her will be more appealing to her than the man who treats her with the utmost respect. In fact, Mr. Right in her eyes doesn't seem real at all. When he came along, this is what she would say.

He Was Too Boring

One of my counselees was an attractive young woman who had been pursued by a young doctor who wanted desperately to marry her. He offered her a world of security and possibilities. He sent her flowers. He often took her to dinner. He complimented her daily on her beauty, charm, and grace. Every chance he had, he would call her on the phone just to tell her he was thinking of her. He treated her like a lady. He opened her door. He worshipped the ground she walked on. She was the apple of his eye. She broke his heart by breaking up with him. Why? Because she thought he was just too boring. He wasn't exciting enough. He was too predictable.

She broke up with him to start dating a guy she considered really exciting. He drank hard and partied hard. He was the life of the party. The women loved him. He was a lot of fun to be around. Even her family liked it when he was around. Of course she came from a chaotic family that didn't really view their chaos as abnormal because it was normal for them. She fell hard for this guy. He never kept a steady job. He couldn't be trusted. He had other women on the side. He drank, partied, and smoked his weekends away. They eventually lived together and fought most of the time like cats and dogs. He would occasionally hit heard but would soon after apologize. They would end the weekend together by making love and making up with all the other mess in the relationship forgotten until the next time.

Did I tell you that her father was also the life of the party? He also drank hard and partied hard. The women loved her father just as much as they loved her boyfriend. She was raised watching her mother and father fight like cats and dogs. She wasn't able to make the connection until after five to six more failed relationships. She began to realize that she was attracted to men just like her father. But she also realized that if she wanted to have a healthy and happy life she had to change the kind of men she dated even if that meant dating men that originally seemed boring to her. It was then that she discovered for the first time that she had allowed herself to be disrespected by men all of her life. She had given herself freely to the Mr. Wrongs of the world all of her life only to have them use and abuse her. And then, if she let them, some of them would come back months later to abuse her some more via what is known as a "Booty Call." The interesting thing about these calls is that the women are just as guilty as the men in initiating them. There will be more on this issue in a later chapter.

She is only recently learning how to receive true normal love from the Mr. Rights of the world who consistently respect the women in their lives by appreciating and affirming them for the true beauties God created them to be. God did not create women to be disrespected by men. He created them to compliment the man as equal partners and for the man to love the woman more than himself even to the point of death. Ladies, if you consider that boring then learn to be bored.

Session Four

1. What do you consider a normal relationship between a man and woman? Why?

2. Do you know women that think like the woman in chapter 4? Tell us a little bit about her personal life and broken relationships.

3. Why do you think some women are drawn to dangerous men? (i.e. the guy serving time in prison, the dope dealer, the pimp, the life of the party, etc. etc.)

4. I use to like dangerous fun men because......(fill in the blank).

5. To obtain a healthy and happy life, what did the lady in chapter 4 begin to do?

6. If you are drawn to the wrong kind of guys, what must you do to break the cycle of mental, emotional, physical, and spiritual abuse?

7. Have you ever allowed a man to disrespect you repeatedly? If so, why?

8. According to Psalm 139:14, what does it say about you as a human being?

9. If you're special in the sight of God, shouldn't you be special to yourself? How can you make that a reality?

10. How can you know the difference between Mr. Wrong and Mr. Right, from a biblical perspective?

Fill in the blank, "I deserve better than what I've gotten in my past relationships because_____."

Things to remember:

1. Look for wholesome qualities in a man, not bad qualities.

2. A father who treats your mother bad is not a positive role model for you.

3. You are loved by God even if your father doesn't tell you he loves you.

4. A godly man is a good man to consider.

5. No one is perfect, but Mr. Right at least tries to be the best he can be.

6. Accept nothing but the best in a man, or accept nothing at all.

Say to yourself, "God wants the best for me. Therefore, I want the best for me."

Notes

Write why you are capable of spotting Mr. Right in spite of your past failures.

Learn to become a good judge of good character

Other Notes

Learn to become a good judge of good character

5

TO THINE OWNSELF BE TRUE

Before Mr. Right comes along, you have to examine yourself. Who are you? What are you looking for in life? How are you planning to get there? What type of man would you like to spend it with? Will he like what he sees when he finds you? To answer these questions, you have to answer them truthfully. You can't try to be something you're not because in the long run the real you will ultimately come out any way to the surprise and maybe even disappointment of the one you're trying to impress the most. You have to be true to yourself before anyone else. What are your strong points? What are areas of your life you need to work on? Where did the problems come from? Why are you the way you are? Why do you struggle with certain things in your life? What are you doing to alleviate the problems? The questions are endless, but questions that can help you see yourself for who you really are. Once you've established the strengths and weaknesses in your life, then you can start working at improving those areas that need to be improved upon. If you're not that good at evaluating your strengths and weaknesses, you may want to consider going to a good psychologist, psychiatrist, or counselor who can help you work through various issues in your life.

Why She Does What She Does

She arrived at my office driving a shiny red BMW convertible. A long leg nicely dressed light skinned African American female with long red hair walks into my office with an air of confidence and grace. She was truly an attractive woman. Her Chanel 22 fragranced perfume filled the room. All of 33 years old and moderately successful in her career, I opened the conversation with "So how can I help you" as I reclined in my chair behind my office desk. She responded, "I don't know how to say this, but I think I have a sexual addiction." Without flinching or changing my facial expression, I asked her, "And why do you think that?" "Because I find myself going on sexual binges that can last days at a time" she replies. "Without being too graphic, give me an example of what you're talking about," I ask. "I can be driving home from work fantasizing in my mind about the most erotic sexual things not able to control my thoughts," she says. "When I get home, I can't wait to invite one of my many male friends over for a little fun in my bed. But after we're through, I feel so cheap, guilty, and empty inside. I then ask him to leave." Then she concludes by saying, "The sad thing about this problem is that I can sit in my living room and begin thinking about these sexual thoughts again and again finding myself back on the phone inviting some other guy over for the same sexual favors." "And this kind of behavior can go on for days before I finally get tired of my actions." "These actions leave me feeling very guilty and ashamed." This is what you would call "Booty Calls" where in this case the woman initiates it. This type of call is when someone calls a potential sexual partner over to his or her home for sexual gratification. This became her chief way of trying to fulfill the emptiness she felt inside.

A closer look into her past reveals that she was raised in a family where both parents were active in raising her. She was well educated. She went to church almost every Sunday. She has always been popular with friends and co-workers a like. She is perceived as a woman of high moral character and integrity. She carries herself in an elegant and respectable manner. She was engaged on two occasions, but broke them off for insignificant reasons leaving both men hurt and confused over the breakups. This has been her pattern over the course of her life.

Nice guys get close to her before she unexpectedly breaks off the relationships. Almost every one of her relationships was preceded by romance and sex. The strange thing about most of her relationships is that the relationships are never really fully broken off. She subconsciously keeps their numbers handy for sexual favors only. She doesn't want them to really get close to her. A closer look reveals that Dad was a very busy man. He spent very little time with his children though he was a good provider. And one important note, in the 33 years of her existence, he never once told her, "I love you." Any time she tried to get close to her father she was met with looks of irritation and agitation. He made himself too busy for her and the rest of her siblings. What she had done as a grown woman was create a personal life that resembled her childhood.

This attractive young lady had problems letting really good men get close to her because closeness with men wasn't something she could relate to. Anytime a guy would get close it left her feeling very uncomfortable and uneasy. She had never known a normal loving relationship with her father. She used sex as an outlet to feel the void and the pain she felt deep down inside as a result of not feeling or believing that her father ever really loved her. To her, sex unconsciously filled the emptiness and pain she felt in the area of love. Of course, she discovered that the emptiness would never go away unless she confronted her father about what she considered a major issue to be dealt with. Once she began taking a good look at herself, she determined to make decisions to change some very bad habits that had kept her from enjoying meaningful relationships. She's finally beginning to enjoy a one on one relationship that hopefully will blossom into marriage now that she's being true to herself. She knows who she is now and why she did what she did. She has released the anger and pain she held on to for so many years that kept her in bondage. She now wants to be that woman of character and integrity that everyone perceived her to be in the first place. Now she's ready and willing to meet Mr. Right.

You have to find out why you constantly end up with the wrong guys. It's really not that hard to figure out if you make the decision to first look back at your childhood. What traumatic experience did you deal with in your life that has left you emotionally cripple? In many cases, it is something back there that has caused you to grow comfortable with your dysfunctions that eliminate the hope of you ever finding or keeping a good man. When you figure your true self out it becomes less complicated in finding out what Mr. Right looks like. The women that figure themselves out are the ones who can generally find Mr. Right. We'll see that scenario in the next chapter.

Session Five

1. What are areas of your life you need to work on, and why?

2. I need to get in touch with myself emotionally and spiritually because......(fill in the blank).

3. How can the lady in the chapter five overcome her compulsive behavior?

4. *Do you know anyone with a compulsive behavior like the lady in chapter five?*
   Please explain

5. *What solutions to this behavior do you find in chapter five? Please explain.*

6. *According to 1 Corinthians 7:34, what is a single woman's number one aim?*
   (Read 1 Corinthians 7:34 to find out)

7. I don't need to crave a man's attention because (fill in the blank).

8. *Why do some not so attractive women, externally, end up with really nice men? Please elaborate*

9. *Why do some of the most attractive women, externally, end up with losers?*
   Please elaborate

10. The best way to attract of good man and keep him is to work on yourself; mind, body, and soul. True or False...Please Explain

Things to remember:

1. If you're considering a serious relationship with a man, ask him the tough questions, financially, emotionally, and spiritually.

2. If a man isn't stable financially, emotionally, or spiritually, he's not the right man for you.

3. You cannot change a man, so stop frustrating yourself trying.

4. If you cannot accept your man the way he is, then move with your life.

5. The only one you can change is yourself, with help from God.

6. Let your inner beauty to be the magnet that attracts.

Say to yourself, "I won't disrespect myself for a man." "I'm far better than that."

Notes

Write why you will not let others disrespect you again.

You are special in the sight of God

Other Notes

You are special in the sight of God

6

WHY SHE ENDS UP WITH MR. RIGHT

Have you ever heard this one: "How in the world did she end up with him?" The real question that the woman is asking is, "How in the world did that unattractive, overweight woman end up with a sexy man like that?" The woman asking the question looks at the woman getting married and she's asking herself, "What does she have that I don't have?" "I'm prettier than she is. I have a nice sexy body. I keep my fingernails and toenails nicely painted and done. I have everything going for me. So how can this ugly woman get and keep this nice hunk of a man?" All right, go ahead and chuckle. You know you've made that statement once or twice in your life. But it's a legitimate question.

Why does she end up with Mr. Right and you end up with Mr. Wrong? Lets take a closer look.

The Average Looking Girl That Attracts Mr. Right And Mr. Wrong

I can remember taking an old high school friend of mine who happened to be a female to my college campus party in the early 1970's. There wasn't anything fancy about her. She didn't stand out. She was not really ugly but she was not really that attractive. She was just someone who grew on you slowly but surely.

When I introduced her to some of my female college classmates, I was greeted by whispers of "You can do better than that." "You two don't even look right together." They actually were saying that I should be with someone with more beauty and style. What they didn't understand was that I was with someone with more beauty and style than they could possibly see. What they didn't know was my friend's beauty and style radiated from within. Her beauty couldn't be measured by her external appearance. She was a woman of great inner beauty. And there are a number of women in the world just like her. The more times you spend with that type of woman the more you begin to see her inner beauty and the more you see it the more you're attracted to it. Of course the average superficial man will try to resist the attraction but the lure for the man is almost irresistible.

He can't help but be drawn to it. A woman who radiates inner beauty is like a magnet to a man who is looking for a good woman.

In the movie Boomerang, Eddie Murphy stars as a successful marketing executive with an eye for women. In walks Robin Givens as the sexy marketing executive who beats Marcus, Eddie's character, at his own game. She's sexy, shrewd, and conniving. He has eyes only for her, until he looks beneath the veneer. As the plot thickens, Eddie's faithful assistant played by Halle Berry tries to encourage him through his ordeal with the sexy maven played by Robin. As time goes by, Marcus finds himself completely enraptured by the inner beauty of Halle's character, almost too late. The attraction was her inner beauty. Rent the movie and see how the story turns out. But it is the inner beauty that keeps the relationship together over the long haul of a relationship. The outer beauty can only lure a person into a union. The external beauty cannot keep two people together in a committed union. I don't care how many face lifts or other plastic surgeries you may have. It is the inner beauty that keeps the man coming back for more.

Consider this. There are several Hollywood beauties that are considered the sexiest women in the world. Yet they go through boyfriends and husbands as fast as they go through a box of ice cream. Outward beauty alone will not allow you to keep a man for long periods of time. Once he becomes bored with your looks, he'll look for something deeper within you. If it's not there, he will become disillusioned and then ultimately disinterested. If a man detects that you are really ugly on the inside then no matter how pretty you are on the outside he will eventually see you as an ugly person. You will cease looking beautiful to him. And this goes even for Mr. Right. He is not looking for a woman with a lot of baggage. However, if you trick a Mr. Right in to thinking you're this sweet docile woman pure as the driven snow, he will try to work with you even after he finds out that you've got some serious issues. He understands that no one is perfect but he's looking for a woman who is trying to work through her issues in an attempt to help her develop that inner beauty from within. If the woman is only interested in the external things of life, Mr. Right will not stick around for any long periods of time unless he finds out after marriage that he's made the biggest mistake of his life. He will at least try to work through the differences with his spouse for the purpose of building a good marriage, which hopefully will last a lifetime. And if he's a spiritually minded man, he will pray for God to teach him how to love his wife is a manner that is pleasing to the Lord. Nevertheless ladies, inner spiritual beautiful is necessary in attracting and keeping the man you'd like to be with for the rest of your life

Session Six

1. Have you ever wondered why so many average women have the good men? If so, give me an example of someone you know, without mention her name

2. Have you ever wondered why so many female movies stars end up divorced 4, 5, and even 6 times before ending up alone with no man at all?

3. According to chapter six, why do so many average and even physically ugly women end up with Mr. Right? Please explain

4. Do you have the inner beauty that Mr. Right is looking for in a woman? Please explain

5. What do you think Mr. Right is really looking for in a woman?

6. What does the woman who ends up with Mr. Right have that the other women don't have?

7. Why do some women seem to attract Mr. Wrong into their lives and how can that kind of woman break the Mr. Wrong cycle?

8. According to chapter six, what is necessary in attracting and keeping a Mr. Right? Please explain

9. I know I need to work on......(fill in the blank)......to really attract and keep a a man who is together, emotionally and spiritually.

10. Mr. Right is going to be attracted to me because......(fill in the blank)...

Things to remember:

1. Most women who end up with Mr. Right have good male role models to compare to.

2. Most women who end up with Mr. Right respect themselves and expects to be respected by their man.

3. Most women who allow a man to disrespect them, don't think much of themselves. They generally end up with the wrong guy.

4. Mr. Right is attracted to fun, confident women. You most work to create these qualities in your own personal life.

Say to yourself, "My life will radiate inner beauty because I am going to work on the inner me."

Notes

Write out what it will take for you to radiate your inner beauty for a life time.

God created you beautiful, so act like it

Other Notes

God created you beautiful, so act like it

7

CREATING REALISTIC EXPECTATIONS

O kay ladies. It's time to take a realistic view of relationships not contrived or fabricated by Hollywood. Before we do, let's look at the unrealistic dream relationships that many little girls grow up believing exists between a man and woman:

1. Barbie and Ken—This relationship is a marriage made on Wall Street driven by dollars and cents. Barbie and Ken are the beautiful couple that young girls have been buying from their very beginning creating a magical world of expectation for young future brides who hope to one day find their Ken. The only problem with this picture is that Ken in the real world often works overtime. He sometimes goes bald and has to buy Rogaine to keep the hair he still has. And many times, he doesn't even listens to his Barbie. He's not able to buy the white house on the hill with the white picken fence with the two car garage in suburbia U.S.A. The disillusionment of this dream world leaves thousands of women embittered for the remainder of their lives here on earth.

2. The Romance Novel Relationship—This relationship plays on the romantic heart strings of women all over the world. It leaves a woman thirsting lustfully for a man who looks good, smells good, talks good, with the creative imagination to leave the woman sensually and erotically at the beckoning mercy of this romantic guru. His charm and panache endures for a lifetime never fading from

the realities of life. The only problem with this picture is that this guy doesn't exist for a lifetime. He may last maybe through the dating stage or honeymoon stage of the relationship. But once the novelty of marriage wears off, the reality of the relationship kicks in. That is when the unrealistic dream can potentially turn into a realistic nightmare.

Take A Good Look At The Reality

Each person brings some type of baggage into a relationship. We all have our flaws. We all have our shortcomings. The question you must ask yourself is this. "Can I live with his baggage, the flaws, and short-comings?" If the answer is no then do not pursue this man for a life-long partnership. In many cases, that person's baggage never gets unpacked.

Some women go into relationships saying, "I know he has flaws, but I can change him." "I know he'll change over time." But what if he doesn't change? What if he gets worse instead of get better? This is a question that many women won't answer before marriage because they're far too busy worrying about their wedding. In the back of their minds, they already know the answer, but their desire to marry far out-weigh their resolve to address this relationship breaking question. In reality, the flaws in a person that you chose not to see in the dating stage of your courtship are the craters that place a wedge in a relation-ship that seemed so loving and so perfect before you said, "I do." In reality, even Mr. Right can sometimes look like Mr. Wrong. So in the realism of life, what sets Mr. Right apart from Mr. Wrong?

Mr. Right is a man who lives by a set of principles that others can appreciate and respect even when others may not completely agree with them. This is a man who prioritizes God, family, friends, and community. He respects women even though he may not fully under-stand them. He nourishes his spiritual side while, at the same time, tries to get in touch with his emotional side. He seeks to provide for and protect those whom he loves while working to be the man of honor and integrity God aspires him to be. His standards are high with his moral compass being biblical in nature whether consciously or unconsciously. Mr. Right understands and accepts his role and responsibility as a man. He either has been taught or has learned how to treat all people with the utmost respect. He consistently aims to improve himself and those around him in his quest to live right before God, family, and all mankind. This is Mr. Right. So don't settle for Mr. Wrong.

Why So Many Women Miss Out On Mr. Right

Mr. Right may not have the looks of a Billy Dee Williams or a Denzel Washington, but if you look real close, his manliness will eventually radiate deep from within his soul. As you get to know this guy, he looks better and better with each succeeding day, week, month, and year that you know him. He's a man of moral character and principle. His priorities in life are in order. And his family is the most important thing in his life on earth. But there's one principle each woman must remember in her quest of ending up with a Mr. Right. First, Mr. Right cannot be right unless your perception of Mr. Right is correct. If the woman's perception of Mr. Right is wrong, she will more than likely end up with Mr. Wrong thinking that she's found Mr. Right. If her perception of Mr. Right rings true, she could end up one of the happiness women in the world even though she knows that a man is not given to her to complete her. A woman has to be happy in herself before she can be happy with anyone else. I know this is a very simplistic answer to a very complex issue, but the true perception of Mr. Right must be accurate. Secondly, your expectations of Mr. Right must be realistic. Know that all human beings are flawed and imperfect, but don't settle for anything less than someone with good moral and ethical standards for living. All people are bound to make mistakes from time to time. But if the core of a person is good, those intrinsic values will be the hallmark of that person's persona and character. His actions will reflect what he is on the inside. Thirdly, the woman must believe that she is worthy of a good man lest she end up with any old guy who wants to be with her. Fourthly, she must examined herself at the core of who she is. She must examine her thoughts, her emotions, her soul, and the spirit within her soul. She must examine every nook and cranny of her existence so that she might have to proper view of what a Mr. Right looks like. Why? Because her view of Mr. Right may be based on male role models who were corrupt, conniving, and emotionally cold. In that case scenerio, a Mr. Right doesn't seem real in her reality. She's use to being used and abused, not loved and cherished. She's use to being abandoned and neglected, not smoldered with affection and admiration. That is why in searching for Mr. Right, you have to deal with your own issues so you can know what Mr. Right really looks like.

If you had negative male role models growing up as a result of seeing your mother or caregiver with all the wrong men, or you just having a very low self-esteem of yourself, you have to make a concerted effort to break the legacy you've historically lived by. You have to rethink and reshape your image of what the right guy looks like. You have to resist the urge to go for the wrong guys that you're naturally attracted to. Mr. Right is not necessarily the pretty boy with the smooth lines, the nice clothes, and the right material possessions. In most cases he's not. Mr. Right is the guy you can count on, the guy that will consistently love you unconditionally. He's the guy that will call just to see how your day is going. He's the guy you can pray with and play with, the guy who wants to spend the rest of his life with you and only you. He's the guy whose career takes a back seat to you. Will it take work to find those qualities in a man? Absolutely. Are there any shortcuts along the way in finding them? Unequivocally no. That is why you have to be in search of those intrinsic qualities and characteristics that let you know that this guy truly is Mr. Right. Does he have a relationship with God? Does he surround himself with respectful and reliable friends? Does he pursue excellence in every aspect of his life? Does he handle his money responsibly? Does he treat you like the queen God created you to be?

Does he understand his role as a man in the world we call society? If he does, then you've found your Mr. Right. If he doesn't, may your search for the right qualities in a man continue, in your search for Mr. Right.

Session Seven

1. If you are generally attracted to the wrong kind of guys, what must you do to stop the negative pattern in your dating life?

2. My dad has been a (fill in the blank) influence in my life. Therefore, I have a tendency to be a (fill in the blank) judge of male character.

3. My dates in the past have generally been......(fill in the blank)......ones.

4. My past experience has taught me that men......(fill in the blank)...

5. What is your real expectations of a Mr. Right? Please explain, and why

6. According to chapter seven, how can you avoid a real nightmare with Mr. Right?

7. According to chapter seven, is it the woman's place to try and change a man?

8. According to chapter seven, what sets Mr. Right apart from other guys?

9. According to chapter seven, why do so many women miss out on Mr. Right?

10. According to chapter seven, what are some of the questions I should be asking myself about Mr. Right? Explain why I you need to answer those questions?

Things to remember:

1. Think before you make a commitment to any man.

2. If your taste in men has been bad in the past, take the time to find out why.

3. It's better to be alone with God than to be miserable with Mr. Wrong.

4. Yes, you are good enough for Mr. Right.

5. Yes, Mr. Right will be attracted to you, if you work on you and your issues.

6. Yes, ask tough questions to just how stable that guy truly is.

7. Mr. Right will not be offended by your questions. He'll have a greater appreciation for you instead of less.

Say this to yourself; "I will find Mr. Right by finding myself." "I will find myself when God becomes my number one partner and friend."

After you find yourself, you won't have to worry about searching for Mr. Right. Mr. Right will find you.

Notes

Write why Mr. Right will find you.

Become a magnet through your inner and outer beauty

Other Notes

Become a magnet through your inner and outer beauty

25 QUESTIONS TO ASK A GUY TRYING TO PURSUE YOU

I have found in biblical counseling that far too many women are afraid to ask tough questions of her suitor or potential husband thinking that she will run him away. Well if he can't answer these questions you should let him run away for your own good.

Way too many woman find out too late, after she's allowed herself to become emotionally bonded a to guy, that she's made one of the biggest mistakes of her life.

So do me a favor and start asking these guys the tough questions so you can make intelligent decisions about the various possibilities regarding a relationship.

1. What are your plans for the future?

2. Have you ever been married?

3. Are you married?

4. Where do you work?

5. What do you think of homemakers and housewives?

6. Do you ever plan on settling down in marriage?

7. What do you like about me?

8. What kind of woman are you looking for in marriage?

9. Are you a spiritually minded man?

10. Do you attend church on a regular basis?

11. Do you give of your time to charitable endeavors?

12. What kind of relationship do you have with your mother? (note: if he hates her, scratch him from you list completely. There are probably anger issues that could eventually be detrimental to your health)

13. Are you a jealous man?

14. Do you consider yourself possessive or controlling?

15. I'm a Christian. What about you? (note: if he's not, don't think that God has placed him in your life so you can change him. Save yourself the frustration and cut your losses)

16. What is or was your father like when you were growing up?

17. Are you anything like your father?

18. What's the longest relationship you've been in?

19. Do you see marriage as a life long institution?

20. Could you love one woman unconditionally for a lifetime? Explain

21. Do you consider yourself a stable man; emotionally, financially, and spiritually? Explain

22. If you are a Christian, how do you know for sure? (Note: If he says, "How can anyone know for sure?" keep your distance, because he's probably not that stable spiritually which could lead to much frustration and confusion on the home front when trying to raise your children in a godly home.

23. Do you consider yourself a ladies man? (Note: If the answer is yes, then run as fast as you can. This guy will more than likely cheat on you. Get away from him.

24. Why should I let you into my life?

25. Why would you make me a great husband?

Notes

Write in notes from the answers to the 25 questions from the guy who you may be considering for the position of Mr. Right. Make sure you go over the answers and comments with someone you consider a close friend and who will tell you the truth about what they think of the guy you're considering.

BUILDING A SPIRITUAL FOUNDATION

I would be remiss if I didn't share excerpts from my inspirational book, Powerful Words to Live By: Inspiration for the Soul to help some of you out there who may not have a spiritual base to build on in becoming the kind of woman Mr. Right is looking for. Therefore, as a footnote, I want you to read these choice daily messages for the purpose of inspiring you to change for the better. If you are already established in your faith, then use these following words to enhance what's already there inside you. If you're interested in purchasing my 488 page inspirational book, *Powerful Words to Live By* feel free to order it at **www.1stbooks.com** or you can order it at stores like Barnes and Noble, Books A Million, or even Amazon.com. So let the spiritual, emotional, and psychological transformation begin, in your search for Mr. Right.

"Everyone who hears these words of mine and puts them into practice is like a wise man who built his house on the rock" (Matthew 7:24)

As The Branch, You Need The Vine!

Jesus said, "Take care to live in me, and let me live in you. For a branch can't produce fruit when severed from the vine. Nor can you be fruitful apart from me." (John 15:4)

I've yet to see a branch after it is cut from a tree live. Predictably, it will die, dry up and become useless for nothing. The branch receives its life from the tree or the vine, if it remains attached to the vine.

Jesus says to His disciples, "a branch can't produce fruit when severed from the vine. Nor can you be fruitful apart from me" (John 15:4). Jesus further elaborates in John 15:15, "Yes, I am the Vine, you are the branches. Whoever lives in Me and I in him shall produce a large crop of fruit. For apart from Me you can't do a thing (when it comes to bearing fruit)." This passage speaks volumes concerning your ability to live a fruitful life with that fruit being "love, joy, peach, patience, kindness, goodness, faithfulness, gentleness and self-control" (Galatians 5:22, 23a). The Bible says, "when the Holy Spirit controls our lives, He will produce this kind of fruit in us" (Galatians 5:22).

If we're not plugged into Christ established through a prayer and devotional life that never ceases through obedience in His Word made possible through receiving Jesus Christ as Lord and Savior we cannot produce the kind of life that glorifies God. Why? Because apart from Christ you will follow your own fleshly ways and when that happens, "your life produces…impure thoughts, eagerness for lustful pleasure, idolatry, spiritism (that is, encouraging the activity of demons), hatred and fighting, jealousy and anger, constant effort to get the best for yourself (apart from God), complaints and criticisms, the feeling three will be wrong doctrine, envy, murder, drunkenness, wild parties, and all that sort of thing" (Galatians 5:19-21 TLB). Apart from God through Jesus Christ, you won't be able to overcome the demons in your life.

Apart from your personal relationship with Jesus Christ you won't be able to control those evil desires that dominate your mind, your heart, and your soul. As the branch, you need the Holy Spirit energy (or juice) that flows through Jesus Christ the Vine with God the Father functioning as the gardener of the world. When you get a chance read all of John 15. It could revolutionize your life.

You see, the reason that so many professing Christians can't seem to kick that sinful habit or addiction, they can't seem to get their personal lives in order, they can't seem to get that marriage on track is because apart from Christ it's an impossible task. Without Christ, the specific kind of fruit that He wants to bear in your life is impossible to produce. Apart from Christ, you can't produce spiritual fruit. You can only produce rotten fruit, which produces rotten results.

Be Careful of the Company You Keep!

Paul said, "…after my departure savage wolves will come in among you, not sparing the flock. Also from among yourselves men will rise up, speaking perverse things to draw away the disciples after themselves". (Acts 20:29,30)

Why are so many Christians falling by the wayside? Why are so many who name the name of Christ succumbing to the temptations of this world? Why are so many singles settling for the worlds best instead of God's best? Why are so many married people rewriting their marriage vows with, "till I get tired of you" instead of "till death do us part?" Because the savage wolves of this world have cunningly convinced sheep of Christ that the worlds' ways and ideas work far better than the ways and instructions of Christ. The advice that many Christians are getting is not biblical advice, it's advice concocted by man.

Jesus Christ told His disciples, "I am sending you out like sheep among wolves. Therefore be shrewd as snakes and as innocent as doves" (Matthew 10:16). The Apostle Paul while addressing the spiritual elders of Ephesus told them, "savage wolves will come in among you, not sparing the flock (of Christ)" (Acts 20:29). The wolves desire is to draw you away from the thing of God that strengthen you spiritually. Paul further stated, "among yourselves men (and women) will rise up speaking perverse things to draw away the disciples after themselves" (Acts 20:30).

Who are these savage wolves? The wolves of this world can be your boss, our closest family relatives, they can be your co-workers, your close friends, your professor, your classmates, and even a fellow church member professing to be a Christian. That is why we as Christians must be very careful of the company that we keep. The wolves of this world are merciless when it comes to your faith in Christ. They don't care about you faith. They care about satisfying their own selfish desires at your expense. And if you're not shrewd as a snake while being innocent as a dove, they'll draw you away from the things of God and devour you into their ungodly ways and Christ-less lifestyle.

Therefore, don't let the wolves devour your. If they don't know Christ as Lord and Savoir, don't trust them and don't keep them in your close circle of friends. Replace the wolves in your life with Christ-minded people who can help you grow spiritually and as a human being. Stop flirting with spiritual disaster by being careful of the company that you keep.

Be Strong In The Lord And The Power Of His Might!

"Our struggle is not against flesh and blood, but against the rulers, against the authorities, against the powers of this dark world and against the spiritual forces of evil in the heavenly realms. Therefore put on the full armor of God, so that when the day of evil comes, you may be able to stand your ground." (Ephesians 6:12,13)

The day you received Jesus Christ as your Lord and Savior was the day Satan and his demons plotted to destroy your newfound faith. Before you came to Christ, Satan had no reason to bother you. Why? Because you were living a life that was pleasing to Satan and his demons. You didn't know Christ. You were steeped in immorality. You followed the ways and philosophy of this world order. Your pursued happiness instead of holiness all to Satan's satisfaction.

But then you found Jesus. Your eyes were opened to the truth. You discovered that Jesus was the only way to heaven and that He wanted you to live a righteous life both personally, professionally, and publicly. This infuriated Satan and so now the devil and his demons scheme against your marriage, your family. Your single life, your educational life, your professional life, and very other area of your life, all because he wants to rob you of the spiritual blessings God has given you (read Ephesians 1:3). The Bible says, "Put on the full armor of God so that you can take your stand against the devil's schemes" (Ephesians 6:11). Satan has lost you to Almighty God and he wants you back. He wants you to return to that old lifestyle you once enslaved to.

As a result of the devils constant scheming, the Bible says, "For our STRUGGLE is…against the rulers (the devil and his demons), against the authorities, against the powers of this dark world and against the spiritual forces of evil in the heavenly realms" (Ephesians 6:12). The devil and his demons are alive and well, and we cannot take them for granted. The battles you face in the various relationships of your life have been schemed up by the devil in an attempt to lure you back into an enslaved life of sin. Satan seeks to control your life for the purpose of keeping your soul from the saving graces and blessings of our Lord and Savior Jesus Christ. As a result of Satan's craftiness, we as Christians are to "put on the full armor of God (Ephesians 6:11a) which protects our hearts and mind against the assaults of the devil through faith in Christ extinguishing any scheme that Satan may launch against us. That is why we must be strong in the Lord and the power of His might! We can't fight Satan and win in the power of our own might. Our strength must always be in the Lord and power of His might. It is through the Lord that we can have strong marriages, strong family lives, strong single lives, strong professional and public lives. Because God is our strength.

Well how can you be strong in the Lord? Paul writes, "pray in the Spirit on all occasions with all kinds of prayers and requests. With this in mind, be alert and always keep on praying for all the saints" (Ephesians 6:18). Make prayer to God something you do "on all occasions with all kinds of prayers and requests" knowing that with the devil constantly scheming to destroy your faith that you have to "be alert and always keep on praying" for yourself, your family, your government, your church, and "for all the saints." Don't be discouraged when Satan attacks. Be strong in the Lord, through His word and prayer, and the power of His might!

By Faith, You Can Overcome!

"…whatever is born of God overcomes the world. And this is the victory that has overcome the world; our faith (1 John 5:4)

It is Satan who constantly seeks to destroy your faith in Christ by attempting to cause you to doubt your salvation, to doubt your ability to live a blameless life before Almighty God. He seeks to steal your joy in Christ through the various temptations that this world has to offer. The Bible says, "Your enemy the devil prowls around like a roaring lion looking for someone to devours" (1 Peter 5:8). Satan seeks to devour your faith in Christ while enslaving you to the things of this world. But he doesn't have the power to do it. We're encouraged to "Be self-controlled" (1 Peter 5:8a). The Holy Spirit in us is greater than Satan and anything the devil may throw at us.

Jesus told His disciples, "In the world you will have tribulation; but be of good cheer, I have OVERCOME the world" (John 16:33a)." What does that mean to you and me? It means that you who have received Christ as your Lord and Savior. "You are of God…and have overcome, because He who is in you (the Holy Spirit) is greater than he (the devil) who is in the world" (1 John 4:4). We've already won the war but we still have to fight the daily battles until Satan is put away for good in the lake of fire (Revelation 20:10). Satan is still loose but one day the Bible says, "the Lamb will OVERCOME…because His is Lord of lords, and Kind of kings" (Revelation 17:14). And guess what? "with Him (Christ) will be His called, chosen, and faithful followers" (Revelation 17:14). Hallelujah! We are overcomers with Christ! And until He comes again, we must remember, "…whatever is born of God overcomes the world. And this is the victory that has overcome the world; OUR FAITH" (1 John 5:4). Until Christ comes again for the final triumph over Satan and this world order, we as overcoming Christians, must understand this one truth, "the just shall live by faith" (Romans 1:17). Therefore, stop living like a defeated foe. You're a winner in Christ. Stop letting sin reign in your mortal body. You have the power to say no to sin knowing that your victory rests in your faith.

And when you live by faith in Christ and His Word, victory in your everyday life is assured. And yes, you can overcome everything and anything that you're presently dealing with in life, when your faith is secure in Christ. Praise God for faith in Christ and your willingness to live by it. Be an overcomer and live by faith.

Commit The Strongholds In Your Life To God!

"Everything is permissible for me—but not everything is beneficial. Everything is permissible for me—but I will not be mastered by anything". (1 Corinthians 6:12)

The Living Bible reads, "I can do anything I want to if Christ has not said no, but some of these things aren't good for me. Even if I am allowed to do them, I'll refuse to if I think they might get such a grip on me that I can't easily stop when I want to" (1 Cor. 6:12 TLB). Thousands of Christians realizing their freedom in Christ have become enslaved to things that in themselves aren't bad. But they have allowed Satan to get a stronghold even in the potentially good things that life has to offer. A glass of wine in itself isn't bad, but a person who has an addictive personality doesn't need to drink wine knowing that it will lead to alcoholism. A pill prescribed by a doctor in itself isn't bad, but a person who begins relying on its effects could potentially end up addicted tot he substance. A person who is weak in the area of sexual immorality doesn't need to place themselves in a compromising situation or location with someone of the opposite sex no matter who it is. Why? Because you do not want to be mastered by anything" (1 Corinthians 6:12).

Satan has gained a sinful stronghold on thousands if not million of Christians because they allowed their freedom in Christ to become Satan's tool to imprison them. Paul says, "Everything is permissible for me—but not everything is beneficial." In other words, everything that you do isn't bad, but in the long run, "some of these things aren't good for you" because you can potentially become addicted to them leaving room for Satan to control certain areas of your life.

Commit these sinful strongholds in your life to God. You must come to the realization that there are some things in your life that you just can't handle. It could be wine, prescribed drugs, certain relationships, foods, shopping, gambling, or any other thing that has your mind captured. It will only draw you away from God instead of to Him. Paul says, "Flee from sexual immorality" (1 Corinthians 6:18) and anything that has a mastery over you. You have to come to the conclusion that some things that aren't necessarily bad just aren't good for you. Therefore, flee whatever it is that has a stronghold on your life and draw near to God. You can do it as you choose to commit the strongholds in your life to God through Jesus Christ our Lord.

Don't Back Down On What You Believe!

"I am sending you out like sheep among wolves. Therefore be as shrewd as snakes and as innocent as doves" (Matthew 10:16)

Jesus Christ sent His twelve disciples "to the lost sheep of Israel" (Matthew 10:6). Their message was simple, "The kingdom of heaven is near" (Matthew 10:7). Jesus told them to "be on your guard against men" (Matthew 10:17). Knowing that men would despise them for what they stood and believed in. He told them not to be afraid of human beings who sought to harm them (see Matthew 10:28), because in the sight of God they were very valuable in their representation of the kingdom of heaven and in drawing men and women to Christ.

When others opposed them, they stood firm on their convictions in Christ. When people sought to intimidate them, they were "strewed as snakes and innocent as doves". This basically means that they were clear in perception and sound in judgment concerning others. They knew what they believed. They lived what they believed. They stood firm on what they believed. And so it is with you. People will try to tempt you, intimidate you, harass you, accuse you, and even harm you. But you must stand firm n your convictions, your beliefs, and priorities to live for Christ by developing a clear perception of people and things around you while at the same time using sound judgment in dealing with others. Therefore, you must set biblical boundaries in your life by being "strewed as a snake but innocent (or blameless) as a dove." If you do not agree with someone else's opinions or statements concerning yourself or what you believe, stand firm on your convictions and faith in Christ. Don't let others back you down on what you believe. It only serves to make you a victim of someone else's beliefs and perspectives, which in many cases do not line up with the Word of God. God did not call you to be someone's verbal punching bag at the expense of your faith in Him. Don't let people take advantage of you if and when you're doing what you believe God has commission you to do. And don't ever apologize for prioritizing God and family over everything else in life.

You are God's adopted child commissioned to live by faith as a witness of Jesus Christ based on His Word. So, don't ever back down on what you believe in Christ by being shrewd as a snake and innocent as a dove.

Don't Miss Your Chance To Enter The Kingdom!

"The kingdom of God does not come with your careful observation, nor will people say, 'Here it is,' or 'There it is,' because the kingdom of God is within you" (Luke 17:20,21)

The religious Pharisee came to Jesus and asked Him, "when the kingdom of God would come" (Luke 17:20a). What they failed to realize was that the kingdom of God had already arrived. When Jesus told the Pharisee "the kingdom of God is within you," he wasn't saying that the kingdom of God was physically inside them. He was saying "the kingdom of God is in your midst" because Jesus was indeed the Messiah they were looking for and that by them acknowledging that fact, then the kingdom of God would come. Due to their pride and rejection of Jesus as Messiah, the Pharisee missed their chance at entering "the kingdom of God". But the kingdom of God is still in our midst through the power of the Holy Spirit still waiting to be brought physically to earth with Christ as our King. So at this present time, it's not with careful observation for you to see because it's presently still in heaven. It's invisible to the natural man though a visible reality in the spiritual realm unseen by the naked eye of humanity.

Jesus says, "All authority in heaven and on earth has been given to Me" (Matthew 28:18). At present, Jesus' reign in heaven over all creation is a spiritual reality steeped in eternal consequences. One day, Jesus is bringing His kingdom to earth for the whole world to see. And only those who acknowledge Him as King of kings and Lord of lords will partake in His earthly kingdom. Those who reject Him will suffer the consequences of their actions.

What we must all understand is that Jesus through the Holy Spirit is within our midst from a spiritual perspective. He's always just a prayer away. He knows your victories. He knows your struggles. He knows your pain. And all we have to do is acknowledge Him as the Savior and Lord of your life accepting His free invitation to join Him by faith in the kingdom of God. God's waiting to hear from you. So don't miss your chance to enter the kingdom through Jesus Christ our Kind knowing that the kingdom of God is within your midst.

Fall In Love With Christ and Your Faith Will Soar!

"...those who hope in the Lord will renew their strength. They will soar on wings like eagles; they will run and not grow weary, they will walk and not be faint" (Isaiah 40:31)

On a scale of 0 to 10 with 10 being the highest score, how in love with Christ are you? Jesus said to the angel of the church in Ephesus, "you have forsaken your first love" (Revelation 2:4). Put another way, "you spend no time with me any longer." "I'm no longer the number priority in your life." When a person forsakes Christ even though they profess Him as Lord and Savior, their faith will wane as well.

What is faith but that which you "hope" for and "what you do not see" (Hebrew 11:1)? Faith is "understanding that the universe was formed at God's command" (Hebrew 11:2). And so, when you get to know God and spend time with God, and laugh with God, and even cry with God, you fall in love with God knowing that your hope for the present and the future rests in Him. It is God who controls your destiny. It is God who will never leave you nor forsake you. In your greatest triumphant and even in your greatest hour of need God is there to love you and protect you no matter what. As Jesus has states, "Here I am! I stand at the door and knock. If anyone hears my voice and opens the door, I will come in and eat with him, and he with me" (Revelation 3:20).

God is waiting for each of us to open our hearts to Him, to spend time with Him, to grow in Him, to serve Him, to fall in love with Him. When you do, your faith will soar and be renewed as God Himself strengthens you through His Spirit to run and not grow weary, to walk and not be faint. Fall in love with Christ and your faith will soar!

Follow Christ For The Right Reasons!

"'You do not want to leave too, do you?' Jesus asked the Twelve. Simon Peter answered Him, 'Lord to whom shall we go? You have the words of eternal life. We believe and know that you are the Holy One of God'" (John 6:67-69)

For a little while, Jesus Christ had thousands of people following Him all for the wrong reasons. He had recently fed the five thousand who had been following Him "because they saw the miraculous signs He had preformed on the sick" (John 6:2). They even wanted to forcefully make Him their king (see John 6:15) thinking that He would continue to heal them and feed them. They weren't looking to follow Christ. They were looking for Christ to serve them while they continued to live whatever life they felt like living. But Christ go them straight on this issue when He said, "I am the living bread that came down from heaven. If anyone eats of this bread, he will live forever. This bread is my flesh, which I will give for the life of the world" (John 6:51). Jesus was referring to His death, burial, and resurrection which would be our payment in full for eternal life in Him. And the Bible says, "On hearing it (the statement), many of His (so-called) disciples said, 'This is a hard teaching. Who can accept'" (John 6:60)? As a result of Christ's referring Himself to the "bread of life," "From this time many of his (so-called) disciples turned back and no longer followed Him" (John 6:66). They turned back to their old lives and their old ways and their old sinful lifestyles because they weren't willing to believe in the Christ who could save them eternally. They only wanted what they could get temporarily from God not what they could get eternally. They had followed Christ for the wrong reasons. Not so with "the twelve."

When Jesus asked His Twelve true disciples, "You do not want to leave too, do you? Notice what Peter said, "Lord to whom shall we go?" In other words, if we don't follow you, who are we going to follow that can give us what you can give? The answer is clear and simple. No one can ever give us what Christ can. And if they do give us something, it won't last forever. It will fade away like the rest of the world.

Your relationship will come to end one day. Your career will come to an end one day. Your life in this world will cease one day. But Peter says to Jesus, "You have the words of ETERNAL life." Peter is saying, Jesus, You have something that will last forever. And so Peter says, we choose to follow You Lord for the right reasons. Why? Because, Peter says, "We believe and know that you are the Holy One (The Messiah) of God."

The Twelve disciples followed Jesus Christ for the right reason. Not because He could heal them or could feed them temporarily. But because He could save them eternally through His words and through His resurrected life. We as believers in Christ must ask the same question. If we turn our backs on Christ, "to whom shall we go?" To whom shall we follow? Jesus Christ is the bread of eternal life. Jesus Christ is the only one who holds the key to our eternal future. Therefore, if you want to get somewhere, get there by following Christ. If you want to know where to go and how to get there, get there by following Christ. And in the process of getting there, never, never, never give up on following Christ for the right reason. Believe and know that Jesus Christ is the Holy One of God able to keep you presently, in the future, and forevermore.

For Once, Live Your Life God's Way

"As for God, His way is perfect; the Word of the Lord is flawless. He is a shield for all who take refuge in Him" (2 Samuel 22:31)

Millions of men and women are angry because they believed a lie about relationships and about life in general. They believed that if they gave the person, place, or thing, they cared for whatever that they wanted, he, she, or it would never want anyone else but them, only to find themselves used and eventually discarded like an old piece of trash. And so as a result, you have millions of people who repeat this cycle of personal demoralization over and over again causing much pain and anger, and they wonder why their relationships and worldly plans end up frustrating them. They don't work out because they continue to make the same ungodly mistakes, apart from God, with horrific consequences. They choose to disregard the instructions of God concerning their own personal lives. But "God's way is perfect." "The Word of the Lord is flawless," God's Word says, "Flee from sexual immorality" (1 Corinthian 6:18). God's Word says, Christians, "Do you not know that your body is a temple of the Holy Spirit, who is in you, whom you have received from God? You are not your own; you were bought at a price (through the blood of Christ). Therefore honor God with your body" (1 Corinthian 6:19, 20). "Seek first the kingdom of heaven and His righteousness" (Matthew 6:33a). When you do that the Bible says, "all these things (your desires, dreams, and provisions) will be given to you as well" (Matthew 6:33b).

The reason that so many men and women are angry and bitter is because they're trying to live life in a way, which is not biblically correct; imperfect and flawed instead of God's way, which is perfect and flawless. The only way you're going to be able to turn your life around is to, for once, live your life God's way by seeking first the His kingdom and His righteousness. God is the only one who can shield you from the hurt, the frustration, and the pain that this world pummels you with, but only as you seek refuge in Him through Jesus Christ our Lord. When you decide to be your own shield and your own refuge by following the ways of this world order for your own personal satisfaction and by disregarding the instructions of God, you take direct hits for your disobedience that results in hurt, frustration, and pain leaving you with anger, bitterness, and hostility.

Therefore, stop the madness in your life. Make seeking God through a holy lifestyle by faith in Christ your number one priority. For once, live your life God's way instead of your own way. "He is a shield for all who take refuge in Him." (2 Samuel 22:31)

Get Some Rest and Stay Focused On God

"Six days a week are for your daily duties and your regular work, but the seventh day is a day of Sabbath rest before the Lord you God." (Exodus 20:8)

Working has become a seven-day a week obsession for many people including those in the church. They rise early and retire late in the evening eating and sleeping work. In that time frame, God gets maybe 15 minutes of daily devotion, if that much, as long as devotion to God doesn't interfere with work.

During the time of Moses, Sabbath rest was instituted by God so that His chosen people of Israel could block out the distractions of life and focus intently on Him. It was God's way of reviving His people in a hard, ruthless world on a weekly basis. In the Old Testament, Sabbath rest was observed from Friday evening to Saturday evening. For most Christians, Sunday was and is observed as a day of worship and a day of rest to Almighty God. Sabbath rest is to be a day in which you and your fami9ly focus on the awesomeness of God while spiritually reviving yourselves to do the work set before you the rest of the week through resting and meditating on God.

Moses' father-in-law, Jethro, in Exodus 18 had to tell him that working from sun up to sun down wasn't good for neither him nor the people he was trying to minister to. You have to get some rest or risk physical and spiritual burnout all because you're not allowing yourself time to rest before the Lord your God. Therefore, pick one day out of the week that you can call your Sabbath rest day and rest before the Lord you God. You need that rest to stay motivated, to stay revived in living for the Lord. If you don't get that rest, you risk spiritual burnout and physical fatigue. So for one day out of your busy week, get some rest and stay focused on God.

God Accepts You Just The Way You Are

"God demonstrates His own love for us in this: While we were still sinners Christ died for us" (Romans 5:8)

In sharing my faith in Jesus Christ to those who don't know Him, one excuse for not receiving Him is raised over and over again; "I'm just not ready." The second excuse is, "I want to get my life together before I make that decision to live for Christ." What a lot of people don't realize is that no one is ever ready to receive Christ. We've "all sinned and fall short of the glory of God" (Romans 3:23). Some people actually think that they have to clean up their lives before they can come to Christ when in reality God is the only one who can clean up a person's life through the power of the Holy Spirit.

God knows that by nature we're sinners. That is why through His great love and compassion for His creation "while we were still sinners Christ died for us" (Romans 5:8). God knows our sinful condition. He knows we cannot overcome our sinful tendencies without the work of Christ in our lives. That is why God demonstrated his Love for us and accepted us just the way we are. And all we have to do is to trust God's promise and free gift of eternal life made possible through His Son, our Lord and Savior, Jesus Christ. By faith in the work of Christ, through His death, burial, and resurrection, the Bible says salvation and victory over sin is ours and a new relationship and a newness of life occurs between us and God.

Let's face it. If it were up to us, we'd never be ready to receive Christ. But God in His demonstration of awesome love towards you says, I will accept you just the way you are. So no more excuses. God knows you're not ready. God knows you need to get you life together. And He's patiently waiting to help you become all you can be, from a biblical perspective, as you surrender you sinful life to Him by faith in Jesus Christ. God loves you and accepts you just the way you are.

God Is Able To Reverse Your Problems!

King David writes, "My problems go from gad to worse. Oh, save me from them all!" (Psalm 25:17 TLB)

Life is filled with problems. And for some people those problems seem to go from bad to worse. However, God can reverse your problems and turn them into triumphant celebrations. David reacted to his problems by turning to God. His enemies sought to destroy him. David didn't know which way to turn. Everything in David's life seemed to be falling apart right before his very eyes. But then he turned to God. David new his only hope for survival in this problem-riddled world was found in God Almighty. David says, "To you, O Lord, I lift up my soul, in you I trust, O my God" (Psalm 25:1). Concerning his problems David writes to God, "Show me your ways, O Lord, teach me your paths; guide me in your truth and teach me, for you are God my Savior, and my hope is in you all day long" (Psalm 1:4,5). Rest assured that when problems come your way, and they will, God is waiting for you to cry out to Him for guidance, deliverance, and pardon (of sin). David writes, "Remember not the sins of my youth and my rebellious ways; according to your love remember me, for you are good, O Lord" (Psalm 25:7). In the end, David's problems were turned around by God into total victory. And the same can be true in your life!

Though you'll have days, months, and even years where problems seem to go from bad to worse, remember, that God is waiting for you to cry out to Him for guidance and direction concerning your problems and your life. As David said, "He (God) guides the humble in what is right and teaches them His way. All the ways of the Lord are loving and faithful" (Psalm 25:9,10). And God's love and faithfulness applies to your life as well.

Don't allow the problems in your life to eliminate your triumphant. Your victories come through God as you focus on Him in spite of your problems. David said, "My eyes are ever on the Lord, for only He will release my feet from the snare (of problems)" (Psalm 25:15). Make it your habit to pray to God for deliverance and guidance as you face your own personal problems knowing that only God can reverse your problems turning them into total victories.

God Is Bigger Than Any Sin You Could Commit!

"…where sin abounded, grace abounded much more, so that as sin reigned in death, even so grace might reign through righteousness to eternal life through Jesus Christ our Lord" (Romans 5:20b-21)

A Pastor calls a member of his church to see how she's doing. He starts by saying, "Hello Sister. We haven't seen you in awhile." "How are you doing?" Her reply, "I've been doing terrible Pastor." "I've been living in sin. I no what I'm doing is wrong, but I just can't seem to stop the sinning." "I've decided to stop bothering God with my sinfulness." "I confess it and then turn back around and sin some more." "I'm just not going to bother God any longer with what I'm dealing with." "He's probably tired of hearing my same old lame confessions and excuses anyway."

Millions of professing Christians use that same rationale every single day in deciding to turn their backs on God all because they feel that the sin in their life is just too horrible and gripping to continually bring to Almighty God. What a pity! The same reasoning is also used by non-Christians who have an interest in Christ but who feel that they're just not ready to receive Jesus as their Lord and Savior. Not because they don't believe in Christ but because they have sin in their lives that need to be dealt with, by themselves, first. Many of us know that the Bible clearly says that we've "all sinned and fall short of the glory of God" (Romans 3:23). But do you know that there is no sin that you can commit that God can't forgive seeing that Christ died for all the sins of the world? That's why Christ died. To pay for the sins of the World! And so, "where sin abounded" the "grace" of God "abounded much more." Put another way, God's grace is far greater than any sin you could commit. Why? Because God knows you're a sinner in need of His grace every single day. Satan would have you believe that God doesn't love you because you're so wretched. But Paul writes of himself, "O wretched man that I am! Who will deliver me from this body of death. Thank God through Jesus Christ our Lord" (Romans 7:24)! God will one day deliver you from your body of imperfection that you now live with. And so, in the mean time, the more we see our sinfulness, the more we see God's abounding grace forgiving us. If you've received Christ as your Lord and Savior, God's kindness now rules in your life instead of His judgment (read Romans 8:1) giving us right standing with God and resulting in eternal life through Jesus Christ our Lord.

Does this mean we should keep sinning? No, on the contrary, we should seek to live righteous before God and man. But is God's grace that continually forgives us, and it is God's grace that eternally saves us. Therefore, stop beating yourself up for your imperfections. Stop wallowing in your sins. Confess them to God and let Him work in your life as your choice to live rightly before Him. God loves you and will always be there for you not matter what you may be dealing with. His grace is bigger than any sin you could ever commit! God's grace truly is sufficient!

God Is For His Heavenly Children!

"If God be for us, who can be against us?" (Romans 8:31)

A recent article that I read suggests pessimism is a habit that permeates our society causing the majority of our population to stress over the small stuff in life, not to mention the large stuff. Pessimism for the most part has become a habit, which cripples the faith of millions of Christian throughout the world. However, pessimism is a habit that can and should be broken by those who name the name of Christ.

There is not doubt about it; God is for those who seek to please Him with their time, talents, and treasures. And so, "If God is for us, who can be against us (Romans 8:31)?" The Apostle Paul is not saying that you won't have hard times or that crisis won't infiltrate your life. He's saying that through it all God is for us, not against us. He's there with us come what may. And that through the turmoils of life, "we are more than conquerors through Him who loved us" (Romans 8:37). And since God is for us, that is why Paul is "convinced that neither death nor life, neither angels nor demons, neither the present nor the future, nor any powers, neither height nor depth, nor anything else in all creation, will be able to separate us from the love of God that is in Christ Jesus our Lord" (Romans 8:38,39).

Lets replace pessimism in our lives with confidence that rests in knowing that God is for us, not against. In fact, meditate on this passage of scripture and repeat it to yourself at least ten times a day until it sinks in; "If God be for us, who can be against us." Stop worrying about your situations and start praising God for the many blessing you now possess in Christ Jesus. God is for you, not against you.

God Loves You In Spite Of You

"Long ago, even before He made the world, God chose us to be His very own, through what Christ would do for us; He decided then to make us holy in His eyes, without a single fault—we who stand before Him covered with His love" (Ephesians 1:4 TLB)

The Bible says, "His (God's) unchanging plan has always been to adopt us into His own (heavenly) family by sending Jesus Christ to die for us. And He did this because He wanted to" (Ephesians 1:5). What this means is that as a Christian, your works of righteousness will never save you. Your sinful nature will never condemn you. For "God chose us to be His very own, through what Chris would do for us" (Ephesians 1:4). We are saved through faith in Christ, not in our works (see Ephesians 2:8,9)

What boggles the mind is that, "Long ago, even before He made the world, God chose us." God chose you not based on how spiritual you were or how spiritual you would become, He chose you just "because He wanted to" (Ephesians 1:5). The ultimate grace of God is that your salvation in Christ is a gift. You didn't earn it. You didn't have to work for it. You didn't have to beg for it. And you don't have to work for it now. All you had to do is receive it by accepting God's free gift of eternal life through Jesus Christ. And the Bibles says, "having chosen us, He called us with Christ's goodness, gave us right standing with Himself, and promised us His glory" (Romans 8:30). God has "decided...to make us holy in His eyes, without a single fault" (Ephesians 1:4).

Some of you feel that you've disappointed God with your life and your actions. But God loves you in spite of you, no matter what. There is nothing you could ever do that would surprise or disappoint God. He already knows your weaknesses. He already knows your personal struggles. That's why He's given you the Holy Spirit to indwell your life to help you overcome those areas in your life that disappoint and discourage you. Remember, God is constantly working in your life to workout His own plan in you for His good pleasure. He knew you and your weaknesses before you knew yourself. And yet, He's declared us 'not guilty.' "He's decided to make us holy in His eyes, without a single fault." So stop beating yourself up. As a human being, you're not perfect, but through Christ, God has chosen you to be His very own, "Long ago, even before He made the world."

God Never Gives Up On You!

"Samson prayed to the Lord, 'O Sovereign Lord, remember me. O God, please strengthen me must once more, and let me with one blow get revenge on the Philistines for my two eyes'" (Judges 16:28)

Millions of Christians are paralyzed by their sinful ways resulting in self-induced isolation from God. They reason with themselves that God doesn't want to be bothered with them since they struggle and in many cases practice sins that they passionately hate. And so, they isolate themselves from God instead of drawing near to Him. A reaction to sin that Satan thoroughly enjoys to see in all Christians.

When you consider Samson, known as a champion of Israel in the Old Testament, the Bible says that "the Spirit of the Lord came upon him in power" *Judges 14:19). God used Samson to defeat and humiliate the Philistines who were enemies of Israel on numerous occasions. "Samson led Israel for twenty years in the days of the Philistines" (Judges 15:20). And yet Samson was one of the biggest womanizers of his day. He slept with prostitutes (see Judges 16:1). He slept with women who didn't worship or know God. He disobeyed God in revealing the secret of his great strength to Delilah, a Philistine whom he had fallen in love with. And the Bible says that after Samson revealed the secret of his great strength to Delilah (his hair) as he slept in her lap, "she called a man to shave off the seven braids of his hair, and so began to subdue him (they tied him up). And his strength left him" (Judges 16:19). "He awoke from his sleep and thought, 'I'll go out as before and shake myself free.' But he did not know that the Lord had left him. Then the Philistines seized him, gouged out his eyes and took him down to Gaza" (Judges 16:20-21). But always remember this fact. God is a God of second, third, and fourth chances. God never gives up on you so don't give up on Him! Samson didn't.

When rulers of the Philistines sought to humiliate Samson, God's champion of Israel, while offering great sacrifices to their go Dagon, in spite of his human frailties, notice what Samson did. "Then Samson prayed to the Lord, 'O Sovereign Lord, remember me. O God, please strengthen me just once more, and let me with one blow get revenge on the Philistines for my two eyes.'" Samson's relationship with God had been restored in spite of his shortcomings during this moment of deep shame and remorse. God never gave up on him. God used Samson one last time allowing Samson to have the last laugh on the Philistines. God had given Samson one more chance. "Samson said, 'Let me die with the Philistines!' Then he pushed with all his might, and down came the temple on the rulers and all the people in it. Thus he killed many more when he died than while he lived" (Judges 16:30).

God never gave up on Samson, and He will never give up on you. He is the God of second chances. Therefore, do like Samson. Pray to go in your weakness and say, "O Sovereign Lord, remember me. O God, please strengthen me so that I might live a life that honors you." "Let me be your champion in representing the kingdom of God hear on earth." The God of second chances is waiting to hear from you. He'll never give up on you so don't give up on Him.

God Never Sets Us Up To Fail

"If God is for us, who can be against us? He who did not spare His own Son, but delivered Him up for us all, how shall He not with Him also freely give us all things?" (Romans 8:31b, 32)

A few years ago, a single woman I know was angry with God for not granting her the so-called "man of her dreams" that she had been dating and prayerfully hoping to one day marry. That same man eventually married someone else leaving his longtime girlfriend emotionally distraught and distressed over her failure to keep her man. She eventually grew angry and despondent toward God thinking that He had set her up to fail when in actuality God had set her up to succeed.

The man that she had been praying for eventually left his first wife within three years of being married, filed for divorce, filed for bankruptcy, lost his good paying job due to his hidden dependency on alcohol and drugs leaving a trail of pain and heartache in his path. The lesson she learned from this experience was this: God never sets us up to fail even if we feel like He has. Why? Because, "If God is for us, who can be against us (or who can defeat us)?" The answer is clear. No one or nothing can defeat us, if God is for us. And so no matter what your perceived defeat may be or may have been, in actuality, God is using that experience in your life for your ultimate success because no one or nothing can defeat us, if God is for us. Always remember that if God "did not spare His own Son, but delivered Him up for us all, how shall He not with Him also freely give us all things (according to His divine plan)" (Romans 8:32)? God loves you, and He only wants what's best for you, from a biblical perspective. God will never set you up to fail if you're listening and obeying to what He has to say.

If God Redirects, You Must Accept

"Many are the plans in a man's (and woman's) heart, but it is the Lord's purpose that prevails" (Proverbs 19:21)

The tendency of many people is to become angry with God when He doesn't answer their prayers in the manner they had planned. Some people had planned marriage, job moves, career moves, location moves, the healthy recovery of loved ones from an illness, the successful start of a business, the educational completion of a particular degree. And God said "no" or "wait" to their plans sending many into a downward spiritual tailspin all because God didn't answer their prayers the way they had planned.

The Bible clearly states, "Many are the plans in a man's (and woman's) heart, but it is the Lord's purpose that prevails" (Proverbs 19:21). Your plans, though important, are secondary to the will of God. Paul says, "It is God who works in you to will and to act according to His good purpose" (Philippians 2:13). And so, the first thing you and I must always ask of God is "what is your will and purpose for my life?" Of course, His will for us is to always live righteously by faith in Christ Jesus, but God has a plan for your life. As a child of God, you're here to fulfill the will of God, and in so doing; God blesses you with the desires of your heart if it is "according to His good purpose."

Therefore, continue to plan for your life, but if it's God's will for you to become something other than what you planned, or to receive something other than what you expected, accept God's purpose for your life. If God redirects your plans, by faith in Christ, you must accept His redirected plan for your life. And with God's redirection in your life, don't get angry or hostile. God is in control of your situation. Accept God's will for your life knowing that "the Lord's purpose will prevail" (Proverbs 19:21).

Keep On Walking!

"Blessed in the man (and woman) who does not walk in the counsel of the wicked or stand in the way of the sinners or sit in the seat of mockers. But his (or her) delight is in the law of the Lord, and on His law he (she) meditates day and night" (Psalm 1:1,2)

Psalm 1 contrasts the walk of the righteous and perishing ways of the wicked. The Psalmist writes that the righteous "delight in the law of the Lord, and on His law the righteous meditates day and night". The righteous live their lives based on the Word of God and do not cave in to counsel of the wicked or stand in the way of sinners or sit in the seat of mockers." What this passageways is that the righteous who delight themselves in the Word of God will be happy, based on their "meditation" in the Word "day and night". And as a result of their delight and meditation on the Word, the righteous are "like trees planted by streams of water, which yields its fruit in season and whose leaves do not wither" (Psalm 1:3). Or the righteous, this is all made possible because they choose to keep on walking in the ways o God instead of the ways of the wicked who have chosen not to follow after the things of God found in His Word. "The way of the wicked will perish" (Psalm 1:6b).

If you are not standing or sitting in the ways of sinners or mockers, it's time to get up and start walking. And when you start walking, keep on walking. Don't let sin keep you from walking in the counsel of Almighty God found in His Word. In fact, the Bible says to "throw off everything that hinders (you) and the sin that so easily entangles, and let us run with perseverance the (righteous) race marked out for us" (Hebrews 12:1a). So what if you've messed up. Throw it off, and keep on walking. So what if you still struggle with bad habits. Confess it to God, turn from those bad habits, and keep on walking. So what if you're not where you'd like to be in your Christian life, "run with perseverance" and keep on walking. "Let us fix our eyes on Jesus, the author and perfecter of our faith" (Hebrews 12:2) so that we're not easily entangled in the sin that tries to weigh us down and distract us from fighting the good fight of faith. Therefore, stop focusing on your sin, but rather, fix your eyes on Jesus sidestepping the counsel of the wicked, the way of sinners, and the seat of mockers. In order to do so you have to keep on walking in the ways of God knowing that by so doing, you will be happy and you will be "like a tree planted by streams of water" firmly planted in the ways of God. So wherever you are in your spiritual walk, fix your eyes on Jesus and keep on walking. You cannot lose spiritually when you keep on walking.

Learn How To Walk By The Spirit

"So I say, live by the Spirit, and you will not gratify the desires of the sinful nature" (Galatians 5:16)

The Living Bible is so practical in its translation of Galatians 5:16. It reads, "I advise you to obey only the Holy Spirit's instructions. He will tell you where to go and what to do, and then you won't always be doing the wrong things your evil nature wants you to" (Galatians 5:16 TLB).

Many people hear that phrase, "Walk by the Spirit" and they don't have a clue as to what it means. In order to "walk by the Spirit" of God you have to first be able to accept God's promises and instructions outlined in the Bible, God's Word. Accepting God's Word requires that you then humble your old sinful nature by resisting the temptations of the world. The Bible says, "we naturally love to do evil things that are just the opposite from the things the Holy Spirit tells us to do" (Galatians 5:17). And the Holy Spirit is not going to teach you or remind you of anything contrary to the Word of God. And so, in order to "walk by the Spirit: of God you have to accept the Word of God as truth. Secondly, you have to humble your old nature by rejecting to do those old sinful things you use to do. Thirdly, you have to obey the Holy Spirit's instructions found in the Word of God, which of course requires you to live by faith. When you are able to do these three things, then you've just learned how to walk by the Spirit of God through faith in Jesus Christ our Lord.

So get in the Word of God and let the Holy Spirit teach and remind you what thus sayeth the Lord for your own individual life. No matter what you're struggling with, if you do not want to gratify the desires of your old sinful nature, then learn how to walk by the Spirit of God.

Learn To Follow The Example Of Christ

"Follow my example, as I follow the example of Christ" (1 Corinthians 11:1)

The Apostle Paul wrote the above statement to Christians who were caught up in what is known as legalism and liberalism. The legalist practiced a lifestyle where you couldn't do this and you couldn't do that, you couldn't eat or drink this you couldn't eat or drink that. The liberalist practiced freedom; you're free to go here and you're free to go there, you're free to eat or drink this and you're free to eat or drink that. Paul explains, "everything is permissible—BUT not everything is beneficial. Everything is permissible—BUT not everything is constructive. Nobody should seek his own good, but the good of others" (1 Corinthians 10:23,24). Put another way, nobody should seek to do whatever he or she wants to do, though you're free to it, without considering how it will affect your fellow man and fellow brother or sister in Christ. In so many words Paul is saying, 'your freedom could cause a fellow brother or sister in Christ to stumble if you're not careful with your freedom in Christ. And so Paul continues by saying "so whether you eat or drink or whatever you do, do it all for the glory of God. Do not cause anyone to stumble, whether Jews, Greeks or the church of God" (1 Corinthians 10:31,32). Do not cause non-believers to stumble in their quest to find God, and do not cause believers in Christ to stumble in their relationship with God. Why is that? Because our primary goal as Christians is to seek "the good of many" (1 Corinthians 11:33) not just ourselves, so that many may come to Christ through us and through the lifestyle we lead as we follow the example of Christ.

Christ spent time with heavy drinkers, prostitutes, corrupt tax collectors, immoral people as well as the so-called "religious people" of His day, and He did it, without ever compromising on His holiness. Just like Paul, He became "all things to all men so that by all possible means He might save some" (see 1 Corinthians 9:22). And we win some through Christ by following His example through freedom in

Christ without offending others, through considering the "good of others" at our own permissible expense.

Christ is our example for a holy existence as we seek to live free in Him through the love we have for others "whether Jews, Greeks or the church of God." Therefore, let God use you so that many will grow in Christ and so that many will come to know Christ, all because you decided to follow the example of Christ.

Learn To Serve The Lord And Not Men

"Whatever you do, work at it with all your heart, as working for the Lord, not for men, since you know that you will receive an inheritance from the Lord as a reward. It is the Lord Christ you are serving." (Colossians 3:23,24)

Your attitude toward marriage, family, work, and education is greatly enhanced when you understand who you are truly supposed to be working for and serving. If you see yourself working for men and/or women in relationships, education, and job situations, your work can and in many cases will suffer greatly as you observe the imperfections and flaws of humanity. If you only see yourself working for men and women, you can become very discouraged with the situations you're under. But when you realize that God has called you to represent the kingdom of heaven and His righteousness, a whole new attitude of diligence and excellence concerning your work is to emerge as the central theme in your work ethic.

Paul says, "Whatever you do, work at it with all your heart, as working for the Lord, not for men." Because Paul knows the tendency of man to work less diligent when a person views themselves as working for another human being who they may not like to work for. That's why when it comes to "Whatever" we do in life; we're to "work at it with all our hearts" seeing that we represent God in our everyday lives, not men. And God is perfect. God is love. God is holy. And God wants us to strive to be holy in "whatever we do" as well. Why is that? Because, "it is the Lord Christ you are serving" (Colossians 3:24b). And one day, as you do "whatever you do" for the Lord, "you will receive in inheritance (in heaven) from the Lord as a reward" (Colossians 3:24a). May you receive a reward.

So make it easy on yourself and learn to serve the Lord Christ in your life and not men. It will make your existence so much easier.

Let Go Of The Anger, and Forgive

"Peter came to Him (Jesus) and asked, 'Sir, how often should I forgive a brother who sins against me? Seven times?' 'No!' Jesus replied, 'seventy times seven!'" (Matthew 18:21,22 TLB)

Anger is an emotion that does more damage to the carrier than it does to the recipient of the anger. Anger, if left unchecked, destroys relationships, and can engulf a person's life like flames of a fire consuming a building. Anger, if not unloaded, can drag a person down into the deepest regions of depression and the darkest valleys of despair. Anger can lead a person down the intersecting road of bitterness and hostility if this ugly emotion isn't overpowered by the act of love and forgiveness.

When Peter asked Jesus Christ, "how often should I forgive a brother who sins against me? Seven times" (Matthew 18:21)? Jesus didn't hesitate to say, "No! Seventy times seven!" What Jesus was saying to Peter is that we should always live with an attitude of forgiveness. Anger towards another person could end up destroying the person who is angry no the person who has sinned. And so, it's imperative that we let go of the anger, and forgive, before it destroys the carrier. It's time for the healing in your life to begin by letting go of that ugly emotion called anger.

God knows you've been wronged. Commit your concerns to Him. Let Him deal with those who offend you. He does a much better job of dealing with them than you ever could. Develop an attitude of forgiveness. And by so doing, let go of the anger, and forgive.

Let Us Love One Another In Christian Love

"Carry each other's burdens, and in this way you will fulfill the law of Christ" (Galatians 6:2)

The Bible says, "if someone is caught in a sin, you who are spiritual should restore him gently. But watch yourself, or you also may be tempted" (Galatians 6:1). To help restore someone who's struggling spiritually and/or physically is an act of love in the sight of God that those "who are spiritual" are encouraged to participate in. But we all must be careful in our helping o others, lest we be tempted in the same manner.

Nonetheless, during this time of the year, remember a brother or a sister in Christ who has fallen and can't seem to get up. We as brothers and sisters in Christ are to "carry each other's burdens" fulfilling the law of Christ which is to "love our neighbor" as ourselves (Matthew 22:39). Why? Because it is only by the grace of God that we haven't fallen in the same manner. Therefore, let us remember to pray for those in need of prayer and those in need of spiritual restoration. Let us love one another in Christian love knowing that "at the proper time we will reap a harvest if we do not give up" (Galatians 6:9).

Live By Faith and Leave The Why Questions For Heaven

"We can see and understand only a little about God now, as if we were peering at his reflection in a poor mirror; but someday we are going to see Him in His completeness, face to face. Now all that I know is hazy and blurred, but then I will see everything clearly, just as clearly as God sees into my heart right now" (1 Corinthians 13:12 TLB)

Millions of people have lost loved ones tragically to various diseases, causes, and situations. Others have felt the sting of divorce even when divorce didn't even seem like a viable option. Many have dealt with loneliness behind a masked smile. Others have been victimized in a variety of ways leaving emotional scars that affect the victims for the rest of their lives. All situations in life that cause people to wonder why bad things happen to good people and hwy bad people seem to prosper while good people seem to suffer.

Paul says, "We can see and understand only a little about God now. "Now all that I know is hazy and blurred" (1 Corinthians 13:12). In essence, if you're not careful, why questions will leave you frustrated and in many cases angry with God because we as human beings want to know the full story right now. But the Bible says that we won't know the full story about the things that happen in our lives until we're "face to face" with God. All we know is that God is in control of everything that happens in the world and in all creation and everything that happens in life is occurring according to His plan not ours. The Bible clearly states, "God causes all things to work together for good to those who love God, to those who are called according to His purpose" (Romans 8:28).

Since we don't know but little about God's plans, we as Christians must live by faith in God through obedience in His Word. God holds the key to our future goals and desires as we seek to live for Him on a daily basis. But to try to figure out why God does this or why God does that is to frustrate yourself to no end. The Bible says, "I will see everything clearly, just as clearly as God sees into my heart right now" (1 Corinthians 13:12). When? When I get to heaven, not until.

Upon arriving in heave, I will enter a perfect environment filled with perfect people and perfect angels who will be worshipping a perfect God in a perfect kingdom. And all the questions I had about life and about the world will be finally answered. I will finally see and understand the perfect will of God. No longer will my why questions be hazy and blurry in my mind. Because in my perfect heavenly state, I will understand why all that has happened in my life has happened, and it will make perfect sense to me.

In the meantime, we must live by faith in God pressing forward to live right in the midst of the turmoil and confusion that presents itself in a hazy and blurred world. But then one day, you'll be face to face with God. "Someday we are going to see Him in His completeness" (1 Corinthians 12:13). Until that occurs, stop trying to figure out why things happen and just live by faith in God through Christ. Things happen. So live by faith and leave the why questions for heaven. Receive Jesus Christ as your Lord and Savoir and you'll get to heaven.

Make It Your Goal To Please God!

"We make it our goal to please Him whether we are at home in the body or away from it. For we must all appear before the judgment seat of Christ, that each one may receive what is due him for the things done while in the body whether good or bad" (2 Corinthians 5:9, 10).

Obedience in the word of God equals faith. Faith that God's word is not only true but also applicable to my everyday existence and every situation in my life. An do, even though the word of God may not sound right to my intellect, my emotions, or my will, I will decide to "Trust in the Lord with all my heart and lean not on my own under-standing" (Proverbs 3:5). I will "IN all my ways acknowledge Him" (Proverbs 3:6a). Knowing that "He will make my paths straight" (Proverbs 3:6b). Trusting in the Lord, leaning and acting on the instructions of the Lord is what pleases God, not what seems right in your own eyes. The Bible says, "There is a way that seem right to a man (or woman), but in the end it leads to death" (Proverbs 14:12). Millions of people are following their own way, which doesn't include Christ not understanding that their way leads to death as ell as a cha-otic and unfulfilled life. Jesus says, "Enter through the narrow gate (through trusting Him). For wide is the gate and broad is the road that leads to destruction, and many enter through it. But small is the gate (of Christ) and narrow the road that leads to (eternal) life, and only a few find it" (Matthew 7:13, 14).

Make it your number one goal in life to please God, through faith in Him and His word. Why? "For we must all (Christians) appear before the judgment ("Bema") seat of Christ, that each one may receive what is due him for the things done while in the body, whether good or bad" (2 Corinthians 5:10).

For those who may not know, the "bema" seat judgment is the time at which all Christians will stand before Christ to receive his (or her) reward based on what you did and how you lived while on earth. Did you live for Christ or did you live for self? Did you commit your whole life to Christ only part of it? Did you raise you children n the fear and admonition of God's word? Did you love your spouse as Christ loved the church? All of these questions will come to light at the "bema" seat judgment. A judgment reserved only for those who have received Christ as Savior. The Bible says, that "if what he (the Christian) has built (in life) survives, he will receive his reward. If it is burned up, he will suffer loss (of rewards); he himself WILLL BE SAVED, but only as one escaping through the flames" (1 Corinthians 3:14,15). In other words, the person who chooses to build his or her life on something other than Christ and the instructions of Christ will narrowly escape hell and the lake of fire. Whew! What a terrible way to enter embarrassment and shame that could await you at the bema seat of Christ. Live your life for Christ so that when you stand before Him He can say, "Well done my good and faithful servant in whom I am well please." Please God by choosing me make His ways your ways in every area of your life. May God bless you all.

Overcome The Laziness, Set Aside The Craziness

"We do not want you to become lazy, but the imitate those who through faith and patience inherit what has been promised" (Hebrews 6:12)

The author of Hebrew warns Christians against laziness, which leads to a falling away from Christ and the things of Christ. Because of laziness, the Hebrew Christians, "though they should have teachers of the Word, they still needed someone to teach them the elementary truths of God's Word all over again" (see Hebrews 5:11,12). Because of laziness, the Hebrew Christians could not digest "solid (spiritual) food" seeing that "solid food (the deep things of God)" is suppose to be fore spiritually maturing Christians who "constantly" (not every now and then) train themselves to distinguish food from evil" (see Hebrews 5:12,14).

If you have become lazy in your Christian faith, you cannot execute God's Word properly in your life because you will not be able to distinguish "good from evil." When you're lazy with your faith, that's when the craziness in your life sets in. You begin going through the motions of your faith, but your actions will reflect your lack of patience and perseverance in the things of God. The decisions you make are determined on whether or not you've become lazy in your Christian faith seeing that God wants us "to imitate those who through faith and patience inherit what has been promised (by God); which in our case is the promise of eternal life, and an abundant life filled with peace and joy as we imitate those men and women's faith of old.

The author of Hebrews also said, "We want each of you to show this same diligence to the VERY END, in order t o make your hope sure" (Hebrews 6:11). In other words, your consistent walk in Christ by faith is evidence of your salvation. If you continue in your lazy state, there's only one way for you to go in the sight of God, and that is back into your old sinful habits that God saved you out of, if in fact you were ever saved to begin with. Also, if you continue in your laziness, you will seek to justify your sinfulness as you fall further back into your old sinful ways of living. Why? Because you will not be able to distinguish good from evil. As a result of continued laziness in Christ, you'll make activities, and job decisions leading to shame, and pain, and sadness, and loneliness, and emptiness, both in your life and those around you; all because you chose not to remain diligent in Christ to the very end.

Going into a new year, don't let that scenario happen to you. Don't let Satan still your joy. Don't let sin control your body as it did before you came to Christ. Don't go on those sinful binges that keep you from God and the things of God. Don't let laziness keep you from spiritually growing in your Christian life. Through perseverance and diligence, get back on track, and get back involved with your church in Sunday morning worship, mid-week bible studies, weekly prayer with a prayer partner, Christian fellowship, and make it a goal to grow spiritually "by constant use" of God's Word. Overcome the laziness while setting aside the craziness.

Praise God For His Awesomeness!

"Sing out the honor of His name; Make His praise glorious. Say to God, 'How awesome are Your works! Through the greatness of Your power Your enemies shall submit themselves to You. All the earth shall worship You and sing praises to You; They shall sing praises to Your name'" Selah. (Psalm 66:2-4)

The greatest difficulty facing the majority of Christians in the world today is the unbelief in the awesomeness of Almighty God. Far too many Christians just don't believe that God will do what He says. Christians have a small view of what God can and wants to do in their individuals lives and as a result they wallow in their lack of faith filled with worry, anger, self-pity, frustration, and utter defeat all because they won't possess the power that is at their deposal through Jesus Christ our Lord. They've chosen not to walk by faith but by sight, which isn't faith at all.

The same God who delivered Israel at the Red Sea as a sign of His awesome power over all nations is the same awesome God waiting to deliver you from the obstacles that are set before you. He" the same yesterday, today, and forevermore. The psalmist wrote, "He turned the sea into dry land, they passed through the waters on foot—come, let us rejoice in Him (God)" (Psalm 66:6). The psalmist further writes, "He rules forever by His power, His eyes watch the nations—let not the rebellious rise up against Him" (Psalm 66:7). And so upon understand God's supernatural powers, the Psalmist wrote, "How awesome are your works! So great is your power that your enemies cringe before you" (Psalm 66:3). Even God's enemies know how powerful He is!

God's saving acts can still be seen today in your life and the life of others. Don't let Satan destroy your faith in God. Don't let your sight limit your faith seeing that "faith is being sure of what we hope for and certain of what we do not see" (Hebrews 11:1). God can work the possible out of an impossible situation if only you will believe in Him by faith. God is awesome! Stop limiting yourself by what you can't see. Live by faith in the promises of God and the godly possibilities that reside in Him through Jesus Christ our Lord. He's still a mighty God (and always will be) who's worthy of our praise. Therefore, praise God for His awesomeness, and start thinking big in His promises and His Word.

Praise God With What You Say!

"Let no corrupt word proceed out of your mouth, but what is good for necessary edification, that it may impart grace to the hearers...Let all bitterness, wrath, anger, clamor, and evil speaking be put away from you, with all malice". (Ephesians 4:29,31)

We as Christians like to categorize sin. Immorality, murder, alcohol and drug addictions are bad sins, while little (white) lies, harmless gossip, a little trash talking, and belittling others is considered an acceptable sin that God will overlook. The truth of the matter is that in God's sight all sin is bad. God doesn't categorize evil. It's just evil. And we should be no different.

That is why Paul writes, "Let no corrupt word proceed out of your mouth, but what is good for necessary edification that it may impart grace to the hearers" (Ephesians 4:29). Our grandmothers and mothers put it another way: "If you don't have anything good to say about someone then don't say anything at all." That should be our motto in life. Take whatever problem you have with someone to the Lord in prayer or "if your brother sins against you go and tell him his fault between you and him alone. If he hears you, you have gained your brother (as a friend)" (Matthew 18:15).

The sin that you commit with your mouth is just as bad as any other sin that's committed by anyone else. It's sin. When your words out people like a knife, you grieve the Holy Spirit of God (see Ephesians 4:30). And so, as Christians are encourages to "put away" "all bitterness, wrath, anger, clamor, and evil speaking" (Ephesians 4:31). Jesus said, "By this all will know that you are My disciples, if you have love for one another" (John 13:35).

Find it in your heart to turn from all types of sin including the ones that pertain to your mouth. Praise God with what you say and impart grace to the hearers of those who hear you.

Prepare Yourself For Battle!

Paul says, "I use God's mighty weapons, not those made by men, to knock down the devil's strongholds. These weapons can break down every proud argument against God and every wall that can be built to keep men from finding Him. With these weapons I can capture rebels and bring them back to God, and change them into men (and women) whose hearts' desire is obedience to God (2 Corinthians 10:4,5 TLB)

Fellow soldiers in Christ are falling by the wayside everyday, all because they go into battle unprepared for the spiritual warfare that awaits them. In the day to day battle, Christians are ambushed by the enemy because they're not preparing themselves to handle Satan and his demons whose number one desire is to destroy our faith and confidence in our heavenly Father through Jesus Christ our Lord. As a result, casualties are high on the battlefield. Marriages are destroyed. Children are devastated by the lack of faith they see in their parents. Christian's relationship with Christ become superficial instead of intimate and deep. The desire to succeed in life becomes driven by the philosophies of our society instead of the teachings of the Word of God and our commitment to honor God. Sin reigns in the lives of those who profess Christ as Lord. What God wants us to do is prepare ourselves for the spiritual battles that awaits us every single day, both inside the home and out, so we can stand as mighty warriors for Christ in every area of our lives.

Paul says, "I use God's mighty weapons, not those made by men, to knock down the devil's strongholds" (2 Corinthians 10:4). Just like Jesus Christ, Paul used the Word of God as His chief weapon to battle the devil. With the Word of God you can "knock down the devil's strongholds" in you life. You don't have to be a prisoner of sin any longer. Jesus Christ has set you free. Your marriage doesn't have to be a battlefield if only you'll apply the Word of God concerning marriage to your everyday life. You don't have to constantly fail in your life concerning sin if you will begin to daily prepare yourself for spiritual battle through the Word of God. The Bible says, "These weapons (the instructions of God) can break down every proud argument against God and every wall that can be built to keep men from finding Him" (2 Corinthians 10:5a). Not only that, with these weapons, we can bring men and women to or "back to God, and change them into men (and women) whose hearts' desire is obedience to Christ" (2 Corinthians 10:5b). That's the kind of power each individual Christian soldier has in their life if only they would take the time to prepare themselves for spiritual warfare.

If you're struggling in your marriage, your single life, your college life, your work life, or your church lie, it's time to prepare yourself for battle. "For we are not fighting against people made of flesh and blood, but against persons without bodies—the evil rulers of the unseen world; and against huge number of wicked spirits in the spirit world" (Ephesians 6:12 TLB). "So use every piece of God's armor (in His Word) to resist the enemy whenever he attacks, and when it is all over, you will still be standing up" (Ephesians 6:13). If you've lived long enough, you know the battle is real. Therefore, prepare yourself for battle. "When it is all over, you will still be standing up.

Protect Yourself From Satan

"Do not deprive each other except by mutual consent and for a time, so that you may devote yourselves to prayer. Then come together again so that Satan will not tempt you because of your lack of self-control". (1 Corinthians 7:5).

In the arena of marriage, Satan is having a field day on couples who have become bored in the carrying out of the intimate duties of their relationship. The husband buries himself in his work. The wife grows cold and frustrated within her marriage. The two grow apart and begin to lead separate lives due to the lack of romance and intimacy within the relationship. There is a breakdown in communication. Satan begins to tempt both husband and wife with non-sexual affairs in the workplace, which could possible lead to sexual ones. Both parties begin to concentrate on the faults of the other instead of the positive qualities that each brings to the relationship. Isolation sets in the relationship where the emotional bond between the two no longer exists. And through it all, Satan and his demons wait in the darkness for the relationship to unravel for good.

This scenario doesn't have to be yours, if you would only follow God's Word on the subject. That is why I suggest you read 1 Corinthians 7 very carefully. Paul says to the married couples, "Do not deprive each other except by mutual consent and for a time, so that you may devote yourselves to prayer" (1 Corinthians 7:15). It is true that a family that prays together stays together. And even though there will be disagreements, the communication between husband and wife will be open as you discuss your concerns with Almighty God. God becomes the central advisor and counselor in you relationship. He gives you the instructions that that you need to make your relationship work. And God says, that "The husband and wife should fulfill his or her marital duty to his spouse" (see 1 Corinthians 7:1-4). Why? "So that Satan will not tempt you" (with others outside of your marriage) "because of your lack of self-control" brought on by lack of intimacy within the marriage relationship. Two things God wants you to have within your relationship; 1) intimacy, on a weekly basis, and 2) prayer, concerning all aspects of your relationship and life decisions. It will keep your relationship strong and it will keep you spiritually strong in your protection against the temptations, which will come from Satan.

Therefore, protect yourself from Satan by following the mandates of God's Word concerning your married life, your single life, and your spiritual life. God's Word concerning your particular situation will always protect you from the attacks of Satan.

Replace The Old Habits With New Ones!

"So now we can obey God's laws if we follow after the Holy Spirit and no longer obey the old evil nature within us". (Romans 8:4 TLB)

Every person who has a physical body struggles with sin in some form or another. The Apostle Paul says, "my new life (nature) tells me to do right, but the old nature that is still inside me loves to sin" (Romans 7:25b). This is the reality of every Christian's experience. With the new nature inside you, you want to do right, but your old nature still loves to sin. That explains why so many Christians continue to struggle with anger, gossip, malice, pride, the lust of the flesh, the lust for power, various mind altering substance addictions, and the like. Why? Because your old nature is still alive and well. Therefore, the old habits from the old nature must be replaced with new habits of righteousness as we follow after the Holy Spirit.

How is this done? First, we must remove ourselves from those people and things that tempt us to act out those old habits. If you're an alcoholic or someone hooked on drugs, you don't need substances around you that will tempt you to abuse your body. If you've got a problem with lust, you don't need to be in a situation that causes you to succumb to your weaknesses. You need to replace those old people and situations that cause you to sin with new people and situations that encourage you to obey the Word of God as you follow the Holy Spirit in the power of His might. Secondly, you need to get involved with a Bible believing church where you can grow spiritually in your Christian life and where you can develop of strong intimate relationship with God the Father through Jesus Christ the Son in the power of the Holy Spirit through prayer and daily dose of the Word of God.

Yes you can replace those old habits within you with new ones as you replace those old ungodly people and things in your life with new people and situations that will help you in your quest to follow after the Holy Spirit and the things of God. Get started today in replacing those old sinful habits with new righteous ones.

Rest Assure, God Knows You're Not Perfect

"There is not a single man (or woman) in all the earth who is always good and never sins". (Ecclesiastes 7:20)

Every person on the face of the earth has a flaw in their character; from the prettiest to the ugliest. It was inherited by Adam and Eve as a result of their sin or disobedience in the Garden of Eden. It's called human depravity. Human depravity says that your character is inherently depraved and as long as you live in your imperfect body there will be the temptation to sin. The question you must ask yourself is "how can I overcome the tendency to sin?" The answer to that question is this; you can't. The tendency to sin in your flesh will always be there (read Romans 7:14-25). There will always be a tug of war in you between the flesh and Spirit. King Solomon observed in his life time that "There is not a single man (or woman) in all the earth who is always good and never sins" (Ecclesiastes 7:20). Given the fact that you inherited a sinful body, you will always have that tendency. However, with Christ in your life, you can grow stronger in overcoming those sinful strongholds that seem to weight you down.

First of all, if you have friends that influence you to do ungodly things, you've got to remove yourself from that bad influence in your life. The Bible says, "Do not be deceived: "Evil company corrupts good habits (1 Corinthians 15:33). I don't care if you've been raised in the church, went to bible study on Sunday, Sunday evening, Wednesday evening, and even small group Bible studies, bad company corrupts good habits.

Secondly, make honest prayer a number one priority in your communication with God. Let Him know that you're struggling. He already knows that anyway, but He wants you to be in agreement with Him that you're weak. It is when you humble yourself to let go of your sinful weaknesses committing them to God that you can begin to move forward for Him in the area of righteousness and holiness. God begins to help you in your weaknesses as you determine in yourself through the power of the Holy Spirit to say no to those strongholds that don't seem to want to let you go. God will resist you if you become too proud to admit that you have a problem with sin. Why? Because God knows that everybody has some kind of problem with some form of sin whether big or small. Remember, we're sinners saved by God's grace through Christ. However, our desire should always be to please God with our life through faith in Jesus Christ.

Thirdly, begin to surround yourself with people who will pray and be there for you in your moments of weakness. Don't fool yourself into thinking that you can handle the sinful strongholds in your life by yourself. You will only be successful as you commit your weaknesses to God and as you seek the prayers and support of godly individuals. When you feel weak, call a godly friend and ask him or her to pray for you.

And fourthly, "draw near to God knowing that He'll draw near to you" (James 4:7). When the pressures of life seem to make you want to scream and you decide to ease the pressure by succumbing to your weakness, don't give in to them. Draw near to God by letting Him know that you're weak and that you need Him. And if you feel bad for feeling these tendencies to sin, it only shows that the Holy Spirit is doing His job of convicting you. However, you're not the only one struggling. Mankind struggles with sin, but you don't have to succumb to it, if people who will pray for you, rebuke you, encourage you, and love you as you determine in your heart to do God's will. Yes, as long as you live in this depraved body, there will always be a tendency to sin. But through the Holy Spirit in your life, it you so decide, you now have the power not to. Praise God for the power as you determine in your heart to turn from sin while turning to Him!

Shine Like A Star!

"Those who are wise, the people of God, will shine as brightly as the sun's brilliance, and those who turn many to righteousness will flitter like start forever". (Daniel 12:3 TLB)

There are millions of people who are seeking to be stars in the unstable world of athletics, entertainment, and various other ventures, which leads only to a temporary earthly reward. And there is nothing wrong with pursuing your dreams as long as it is not at the expense of eternal stardom that can only be found by turning others to righteousness in God through Jesus Christ our Lord.

God wants each of His children in Christ to "shine as brightly as the sun's brilliance" and to "glitter like start forever." God wants you to be a star, but from a biblical perspective. He wants you to live your life based on biblical principles standing firmly on His Word based on faith in Jesus Christ and the promises outlined in His holy book, the Bible. And so, by prioritizing God's will for your life by becoming His witness to the world, which means to live for Him, obey Him, praying to Him, sharing your faith in Him to others, "turning many to righteousness" as a result of Him, you become a star that shines and glitters in His presence "forever." Not temporarily, but forever! By sharing our Lord with others, you can be a true star, shining brightly in the sight of God! Today, be a witness for Christ, and shine forever like a star!

Spiritual Growth Takes Time

"...He who began a good work in you will carry it on to completion until the day of Christ Jesus" (Philippians 1:6b)

In order to build a building, a company calls in an architect and builder. The architect draws up the blueprints and the builder constructs the building in accordance to the blueprint design. Before the work is started, an accountant is called in to monitor the progress of the construction based on cost. The accountant or project manager lists the construction under one of three processes: 1) Raw material, 2) Work in Process, or 3) Completed Work. In all, everyone involved knows that the completion of the construction will take much time. And so it is with God, the architect, builder, and finisher of our faith. He counted the cost of His human construction and paid the debt with Jesus the Christ.

God has designed you to be "fearfully and wonderfully made" (Psalm 139:14). "All the days ordained for you (His adopted children) were written in His (work) book (the book of life) before one of us came to be" (see Psalm 139:16). His blueprint is the Word of God with God Himself serving as architect, builder, and project manager of each one of His constructions. Total completion of His constructions will end up in the finished work category, complete with new immortal and imperishable bodies on "the day of the Lord" (see 1 Corinthians 15:51-54). The day, known as the Rapture, when Jesus Christ will come back for His church, when all of God's chosen constructions will finally receive their brand new immortal, imperishable bodies designed perfectly to dwell with Jesus forever and ever and ever. Until that time comes, we on earth are still considered raw material, or a work in process. And guess what? God who began a good work in you will carry it on to completion. But praise God! The payment of the construction has already been prepaid by Christ. We've been prepaid for even though God's work in us hasn't been completed. We're a work in process. But one day it will be complete with God being the author and finisher of our faith.

So just remember, God I not through with you yet. He still has to complete His work in you. Therefore, don't give up on yourself when you try to run in your faith even though you're still learning to crawl in the process of spiritual growth. Spiritual growth takes a lot of time. But God the author, the finisher, the architect and builder of your faith; He will carry His work out in you "until the day of Jesus Christ." Do don't rush yourself in becoming a spiritual giant. Spiritual growth takes time.

Stop Burdening Yourself! Commit Yourself To God!

"Commit your way to the Lord, trust also in Him, and He will do it". (Psalm 37:5)

The word "commit" in the context of this passage means to roll your burdens on the Lord. Put another way, while your burdens may be hard for you to bear, they are never too great for Almighty God to handle. But Satan would have you believe that God doesn't care about your burden or your cares causing many Christians to live in a constant state of anxiety, weariness, and fear instead of faith filled with peace and joy. Satan wants you to become so busy and entangled with the affairs of this world in the pursuit of education, career advancement, financial and material prosperity that you have not time for yourself let alone God. You become so inundated with trying to make ends meat that you forget to roll your burdens and desires onto the Lord leaving yourself weary and heavy-laden because you end up doing everything in your own strength instead of the strength of omnipotent God.

The Bible says, "Commit your way to the Lord, trust also in Him, and He will do it" (Psalm 37:5). Roll your burdens on the Lord and leave them there. Trust God to answer your prayers, and "He will do it." Now remember, when it comes to trusting God to handle your burdens He will, but it may not be in the manner you were expecting. God will deal with your burdens in His own way in His own time. Proverbs 16:3 says, "Commit your works to the Lord, and your plans will be established." But also remember that "The mind of man plans his way, but the Lord directs his steps" (Proverbs 16:9). God wants your plans and ways to always glorify Him. If not, God will redirect your plans until they do.

God is waiting for you to roll your burdens onto to Him so that you will make the time to know Him, grow in Him, and serve Him. And when you commit yourself and your ways to God, the Lord will direct your steps so that you may become the God-fearing, soul-winning child of God that He's called you to be. Serving God starts with committing yourself to Him, which includes receiving Jesus Christ as your Lord and Savior. Therefore, stop trying to do everything in your own strength and start rolling your burdens and desires on the Lord. Let Him do it for you as you seek to live for Him in righteousness and in truth.

Stop Running From God!

"Let us throw off everything that hinders and the sin that so easily entangles, and let us run with perseverance the race marked out for us". (Hebrews 12:1b)

Far too many Christians put on the performance of their lives on the Sundays they decide to show up at church. They smile and laugh and pretend to praise God masking the sin and spiritual inconsistencies that they've allowed to dictate their lives. When the troubles of lies visits them, they're not able to play off their lack of faith in Christ, and so, they just stay at home playing right into the hands of Satan. Instead of becoming angry with themselves and the devil, they blame God for their plight in life sinking them deeper in the quagmire of sin and unbelief pretending to be spiritual giants of the Christian faith.

The Bible says, "let us throw off everything that hinders and the sin that so easily entangles"(Hebrews 12:1). In other words, you can't expect to be a spiritually mind person if you continue to flirt and dabble in sin and prioritize everything but God. That is why the Bible says, "Let us run with perseverance the race marked out for us" (Hebrews 12:1). But you can't run a spiritual race without throwing off sinful addictions and habits that will consistently weigh you down. What far too many people are doing is actually running to the things of Satan instead of the things of God seeking to justify their hypocrisy by going to church on Sunday. And so, in so many words the writer is saying STOP RUNNING FROM GOD and start running with perseverance the holy race that God has laid out for us through Jesus Christ. Stop playing with God and start living for God. The Bible says, "Do not be deceived, God cannot be mocked" (Galatians 6:7).

If you really want to develop a strong spiritual life without losing heart along the way, then stop running from God and start running the race that God has set before us. May you choose to live by faith by first throwing off everything including the sin that keeps you from living a life that is pleasing to God. Secondly, make a daily time and place for the Word of God and prayer. In other words, build your life around the Word of God by faith in Jesus Christ. Stop running from God and start running the race God has set before you.

Stop Worrying Over Things You Have No Control Over!

"And besides, what's the use of worrying? What good does it do? Will it add a single day to your life? Of course not! And if worry can't ever do such little things as that, what's the use of worrying over bigger things?" (Luke 12:25-26 TLB)

Think about it. What does worrying really accomplish? Does it help you become a better Christian? Does it help you lose weight? Does it help your health improve? Does it help bring in more money? Does it help you in your relationships with others? Does it help you become a better parent? Does it help you at being a better employee? Of course all the answer to the above questions is no. "Of course not!"

Jesus Christ commands us not to worry. Jesus says, "All mankind scratches for its daily bread, but your heavenly Father knows your needs. He will always give you all you need from day to day if you will make the Kingdom of God your primary concern" (Luke 12:30,31 TLB). Have you made seeking first the kingdom of God and His righteousness your primary concern in your everyday life? If you do, Jesus says, you have no need or time to worry over things you cannot control anyway. Remember, God is in control or life, not you. God has given you the capacity to work and plan responsibly, but you have no control over the future or its outcome. God is in control of that. As a result of that fact, God wants us to live by faith in Him through Christ, which sets us free from the anxiety, and worry that is caused by lack of faith in a sovereign God in control of everything in and around our lives.

And so, as Jesus said, "what's the use of worrying (if God's in control)?" "What good does it do (if God's in control)?" That's the whole point! Worry is pointless to those who are to live by faith in Christ, because God is in control! The just (those who know Christ) shall live by faith because it is by faith that frees us from worry.

Therefore, plan and work responsibly, but commit all your plans and works to Almighty God by faith knowing that He's the only one in control of life and the life to come. Faith in God through Christ will set you free from pointless worry that accomplishes nothing.

The Lord Is Your Shepherd!

"Because the Lord is my Shepherd, I have everything I need! He lets me rest in the meadow grass and leads me beside the quiet streams. He restores my failing health. He helps me do what honors Him the most". (Psalm 23:1-2 TLB)

David understood God's place in His life. God was his Shepherd and he knew that God would not always give him what he wanted, but He knew God would give him what he needed. He knew that God would give him rest in a place and environment that would refresh and replenish his soul as God directed his life down the path that He wanted him to go.

David saw himself as a sheep led by Almighty God. A sheep is an animal easily led astray, easily confused, easily devoured, making it easy prey for the wolves of the world. That is why David allowed God to lead him as his shepherd. Because in God, David found rest, guidance, restoration, and the help he needed to live his life honorably before God; and you can to. You don't have to do things in your own strength if you allow God to lead you through His Word.

God wants to be the Shepherd of your life through Jesus Christ. Jesus said, "My sheep hear My voice, and I know them, and they follow Me. And I give them eternal life, and they shall never perish" (John 10:27, 28a). David said, "Even when walking through the dark valley of death I will not be afraid, for You (God) are close beside me, guarding, guiding all the way" (Psalm 23:4).

God is our Shepherd walking beside us every step of the way. And God never leaves us or forsakes us. He's always there guarding and guiding us in the direction that He would have us to go. Therefore, let God be the Shepherd of your life. Stop resisting His leading. Let Him lead you. Let Him guide you. Let Him help and protect you in your quest to honor Him knowing that the Lord is your Shepherd for which you shall never be in need.

The Way Of The Lord Is Fair!

"...the children of your people say, 'The way of the LORD is not fair.' But it is their way which is not fair! When the righteous turns from his righteousness and commits iniquity, he shall die because of it" (Ezekiel 33:17,18)

A Christian man chose not to listen to sound biblical advice concerning the lifestyle he was leading. He caroused primarily with non-believing women resulting in sexual activity. And though he attended church regularly on Sundays, he spent very little time in prayer, no time in the study of God's Word, and very little time fellowshipping with other believers in Christ.

When his world fell apart in that he lost his job, lost his home, lost all his worldly possessions resulting in an emotional and physical breakdown, his so-called friends that he drank with and partied with weren't there to help him. It was at this time that he shook his fist at God and said, "It's not fair God!" "It's not fair!" This man expected his so-called friends to bail him out of his troubles because he had more faith in them than he had in Almighty God. God was his last resort.

We as Christians must follow the instructions of God instead of the philosophy of the world. God's ways are fair. It is the world that will let you down. Jesus said, "everyone who hears these words (instructions) of mine and puts them into practice is like a wise man who built his house on the rock" (Matthew 7:24). "But everyone who hears these words (instructions) and does not put them into practice is like a fool-ish man who built his house on sand" (Matthew 7:26). Which one are you?

The Bible says it is our ways that aren't fair, not Gods. For "when the righteous turns from his (or her) righteousness (based on the Word of God) and commits iniquity, he (or she) shall die (or suffers greatly) because of it!" God doesn't make you commit or choose unrighteous acts or decisions. But you will suffer the consequence of your unrighteousness. Therefore, it is not God who is unfair, it is our unrighteous ways. Today, be like the wise man that built his house on the rock of

Christ putting into practice His instructions for daily living. Turn away from all unrighteousness and experience God's fairness through righteous living by faith in Jesus Christ.

There's Always Room For Improvement

"Examine yourselves. Are you really Christians? Do you pass the test? Do you fell Christ's presence and power more and more within you? Or are you just pretending to be Christians when actually you aren't al all?" (2 Corinthians 13:5 TLB)

To improve upon a life, most people are raised to get a good education, to surround themselves with positive people and positive experiences for the purpose of building a "successful" life complimented by a "successful" career or vocation. All things that should be applauded, but all things that can never bring you eternal success, eternal peace, or eternal happiness. That is why we must examine ourselves concerning eternal things. That examination starts with our relationship with Christ. Have we received the free gift of eternal life that's only provided through the blood of Christ? Do we know for sure where we will spend eternity? Are you really a Christian? And after answer those three questions, did you pass the test? If you did, praise God! But guess what? There's always room for improvement.

Paul concludes his letter to the Corinthians by saying, "Aim for perfection, listen to my appeal, be of one mind, live in peace. And the God of love peace will be with you" (2 Corinthians 13:11). If you know that you're a Christian, all the more reason to examine your weaknesses committing them to God as you "aim for perfection" in your never ending quest to improve in your ever growing spiritual lie here on earth. The Living Bible translates it this way, "He happy. Grow in Christ. Pay attention to what I (Paul) have said. Live in harmony and peace. And may the God of love and peace by with you" (2 Corinthians 13:11 TLB). By the grace of God, may we always "aim for perfection" knowing that there is always room for improvement as we continually examine ourselves.

Through Christ, You Have The Power To Be Set Free!

"If the Son (Jesus Christ) therefore shall make you free, you shall be free indeed" (John 8:36)

Whatever your weakness is, don't let Satan trick you into thinking that you can't beat it. Satan would have you think that your weaknesses will always overwhelm you, will always defeat you, and will always hold you captive in spite of the salvation and power that resides in the Son of God, Jesus Christ.

Jesus Christ Himself said, "If the Son shall make you free, you shall be free indeed" (John 8:36). Well guess what? If you've received Jesus Christ as your Lord and Savior, the Son of God has set you free! As an adopted child of God, you now have the power to be set free from any sin that wrestles against your flesh through the power of the Holy Spirit that now resides in your very soul. As a Christian, Jesus Christ has set you free. Therefore, you are free indeed. So walk with the King in the power of His might. Through Christ, you have the power to be set free.

We Owe God A Life Of Undivided Devotion

"We must all stand before Christ to be judged and have our lives laid bare—before Him. Each of us will receive whatever he deserves for the good or bad things he has done in his earthly body". (2 Corinthians 5:10)

The Bible speaks of two doctrines that compliment each other; the doctrine of salvation and the doctrine or rewards. The doctrine of salvation addresses the eternal salvation and security of a believer based on God's grace through faith in Jesus Christ; grace being the unmerited favor of God bestowed upon all who receive Jesus Christ by faith apart from works (see Ephesians 2:8,9). God's saving grace is not based on a person's good works. It is based on the death, burial, and resurrection of Jesus Christ. Therefore, the doctrine of salvation addresses God's gift of eternal life freely given to all who accept it and receive it. The doctrine of rewards, however, addresses the rewards that a believer in Christ will receive after standing before Christ at what is known as the "Bema Seat Judgment" of believers. Put another way, once you've lived you life here on earth as a believer in Christ, you will eventually depart and spend the rest of eternity with the King of kings and Lord of lords, Jesus Christ. While in heaven, the Bible says, that all believers will stand before the Lord, not to see if you're going to hell or not, you've made it to heaven, but to see what rewards you will receive as a result of the life you lived while on earth. The Bibles says, "we (Christians) must all stand before Christ (at the Bema Seat) to be judged (for our earthly works) and have our lives laid bare—before Him. Each of us (Christians) will receive whatever (rewards or loss of rewards) he deserves for the good or bad things he has done in his earthly body" (2 Corinthians 5:10). As a result of this impending awards always in everything we do, whether we are here in this body or away from this body and with Him I heaven" (2 Corinthians 5:9). God wants the honor of rewarding each of us with heavenly rewards. But in order for Him to do that, we own God a life of undivided devotion because o the love He first showed toward us through the sacrifice of Jesus on the cross.

Your salvation is not going to be the issue when you stand before Christ at the Bema Seat judgment. However, the rewards that you will or will not receive will. The Bible says, "There is going to come a time of testing at Christ's Judgment Day.... Everyone's work will be put through the fire so that all can see whether or not it keeps its value...Then every workman (you) who has built on the foundation with the right materials (the Word of God), and whose work still stands, will get his (or her) pay (reward). But if the house he (or she) has built burns up, he (or she) will have great loss (of rewards) escaping through a wall of flames" (1 Corinthians 3:13-15). You'll make it to heaven while losing most if not all the rewards God had intended to give to you all because you chose not to live your life devoted to Him.

Therefore, avoid the great loss of rewards in heaven that some believers will face, and commit your life as Christian to undivided devotion to God through Jesus Christ our Lord. We owe God a life of undivided devotion so that he can have the honor and privilege of blessing us with great rewards, which await us in heaven.

We're Not Here To Condemn The World

Jesus said, "For God did not send His Son into the world to condemn the world, but to save the world through Him" (John 3:17)

We as Christians are to be the seasoning in the world that gives it flavor. Without the Holy Spirit, and us the world is tasteless. That's why we're not to just sit back in our ivory towers and condemn those who are lost and confused concerning the ways of God.

For those who may not know, people who don't know Christ as their personal Lord and Savior are supposed to sin. "Sinner" is their job description. They're expected to commit adultery, theft, murder, and everything else associated with sin. Whether we like it or not, that's the reality that every Christian must live with.

When Jesus hung on the cross, He said, "Father, forgive them, for they do not know what they are doing" (Luke 23:24). Paul wrote to the Christians in Ephesis, "Once you were under God's curse, doomed forever for your sins. You went along with the crowd and were just like all the others, full of sin, obeying Satan, the mighty prince of the power of the air, who is at work right now in the hearts of those who are against the Lord" (Ephesians 2:1,2 TLB). And so, since God knows that we were born into sin, the Bible says, "God id not send His Son into the world to condemn the world, but the save the world through Him" (John 3:17). Well the same goes for us who know Christ as Savior. We are not here to condemn those in the world but to share the good news of Christ in an attempt to save those in the world through Him.

Therefore, expect people who don't know Christ to live like they don't know Christ. In the meantime, you who know Christ go and share the good news of Christ to those who are in need of Christ. Pray that God will make them aware of their sinfulness and their need for salvation. Let your life and your actions reflect the mind and life of Christ knowing that we're not here to condemn the world but to live and share the good news of Christ in an attempt to save those in the world through Christ. And may we be the witnesses of Christ that God has commanded us to be in a world desperately in need of salvation.

With God, You're Never Alone

"The Lord Himself goes before you and will be with you; He will never leave you nor forsake you. Do not be afraid; do not be discouraged". (Deuteronomy 31:8)

Have you ever felt alone in your life? So alone that you felt that you were carrying the weight of the world on your shoulders with no one to help you fight the good fight of faith and with no one who really cares? Have you ever felt afraid of facing the future not knowing where the future would lead you causing you great distress and discouragement? When these moments occur in your life, just remember, with God, you're never alone.

Joshua, the man chosen to succeed Moses in leading the Israelites into the promise land, feared leading God's people without Moses by his side to guide him and direct him, all because he didn't know what the future held for him in the promise land. And yet, God used Joshua mightily as he realized one fact. God would always be with him in spite of the oppositions he would face. Before Moses passed away, he told Joshua, "Be strong and courageous, for you must go with this people into the land that the Lord swore to their forefathers as their inheritance" (Deuteronomy 31:7). Moses knew that God would never forsake Hid people and that God would never desert them. Guess what? You must realize the same thing as you seek to live for Him. God wants you to be strong in the Lord and the power of His might. He doesn't want you thinking that you're going through life all by yourself because you're not.

As you go through life, "The Lord Himself goes before you and will be with you" (Deuteronomy 31:8a). So "Do not be afraid; do not be discouraged" (Deuteronomy 31:8b). With God, you never have to feel alone. You never have to carry the weight of the world on your shoulders. And you never have to face the future by yourself. That is why with God, you're never alone. Praise be to God! With Him, you're never ever alone!

You Are More Than A Conqueror In What You Believe!

"I am convinced that neither death nor life, neither angels nor demons, neither present nor the future, nor any powers, neither height nor depth, nor anything else in all creation, will be able to separate us from the love of God that is in Christ Jesus our Lord" (Romans 8:38, 39).

The Apostle Paul asks a very important question to all believers in Christ of the then known Roman world, "Who shall separate us from the love of Christ" (Romans 8:35a). He came up with the only conceivable answer. Nothing can separate from the love of God. Paul asks, "Shall trouble or hardship or persecution or famine or nakedness or danger or sword" (Romans 35b). His answer was a resounding, "No, in all these things we are more than conquerors through Him who loved us" (Romans 8:37).

The picture that Paul paints of believers seeking to live for Christ is an awesome one. We are spiritual warriors representing the kingdom of God on a mission to spread to good news of Jesus the Christ to all who will listen against the forces of evil and darkness in the world. That is our great commission to the world mandated by Jesus Himself (see Matthew 28:16-20). But we are to accomplish this task with an attitude of love both for one another in Christ and the world as a whole. Will there be opposition to the gospel message of Christ? Absolutely. Will there be retaliation for your faith amongst family members, co-workers, neighbors, and society as a whole? Without question. But through it all, the Bible says "we are more than conquerors through Him who loved us" (Romans 8:37). And as a result of God's love for you, there is nothing that can separate you from the love of God.

During those special times of the year when family members travel from miles around to come together in love, God gives you the greatest opportunity to be more than a conqueror for Christ by putting your Christian life on display for all to see. Some will joke about your faith. Some will question you about your faith. Others will ignore you all together concerning your faith. But some will be drawn to you as you stand firm as a mighty warrior in your faith. And not matter what happens, nothing will be able to separate you from the love God that is in Christ Jesus our Lord.

Always remember, that the safest place for any Christian to be is in the center of God's will, and that is where you are when you choose to stand firm in your faith for Him. And so, as you spend time with family members neighbors, co-workers, and friends, stand firm on what you believe in Christ knowing that nothing can separate you from the love of God that is in Christ Jesus our Lord; nothing at all.

You Can Make It Through The Grind!

"The Spirit helps us in our weakness. We do not know what we ought to pray for, but the Spirit Himself intercedes for us with groans that words cannot express. And He who searches our hearts (God the Father) knows the mind of the Spirit, because the Spirit intercedes for the saints in accordance with God's will" (Romans 8:26-27)

If your life is filled with peace and joy, then praise God! If your life is filled with uncertainty, disappointment, pain, and sorrow, or all of the above, you still have a lot to praise God for. Because God is working in your life, you can make it through the grind. When you're feeling low and weak, you can praise God knowing that the Spirit of God "helps us in our weakness." You may be fretting over you future, your finances, your relationships, your crumbling marriage, your job, your children, your health, your personal struggles, but praise God! You can make it through the grind!

Even when we're so emotionally and physically weak and "We do not know what we ought to pray for" we can praise God because "the (Holy) Spirit Himself intercedes (perceptively and intuitively) for us with groans that words cannot express" (Romans 8:26b). The Holy Spirit knows your joy, your uncertainty, your disappointment, your pain, and your sorrow. The Holy Spirit always comes to our rescue when no one else does. Even when people have written you off, the Holy Spirit is still there for you. And even though the Holy Spirit expresses to God the Father "groans that words cannot express," God our Father knows exactly what the Holy Spirit is expressing concerning you and me. And in this passage we see the Trinity of God working beautifully on our behalf. God the Father, "searches our hearts" while also knowing "the mind of the (Holy) Spirit" not to mention the fact that Jesus Christ is continually interceding on our behalf in heaven. The Bible says, "He (Jesus) always lives to intercede for them (those who have received Christ as Lord and Savoir).

So no matter what you're going through or dealing with, the Trinity of God is at work on your behalf with the Holy Spirit voicing your requests to our heavenly Father even though you at times don't know what to pray for in the midst of the grind of life. But you've got a lot to be thankful for. God never writes you off. He's always there to help you and encourage you. You're not a loser in His sight seeing that you've been "fearfully and wonderfully made" (Psalm 139:14) by Him. You can praise God in the midst of your current situation, because He's always working on your behalf. He'll never let you down. So don't give up on your quest to live for Him. For with God, you can make it through the grind.

You Cannot Successfully Run From God!

"The Lord sent this message to Jonah, the son of Amittai: Go to the great city of Nineveh, and give them this announcement from the Lord: 'I am going to destroy you, for your wickedness rises before me; it smells to highest heaven.' But Jonah was afraid to go and ran away from the Lord" (Jonah 1:1-3a TLB)

Many of you were raised in churches where the gospel of Jesus Christ was preached almost every Sunday. You were taught the difference between right and wrong from a biblical perspective. You know that God hates sin. You were encouraged to always make God the number priority of you life. You believe, without a shadow of a doubt, that Jesus Christ is the only way to heave. You also believe that God wants you to fellowship with other Christians on a weekly basis to keep you motivated and inspired to live the life that God has commissioned you to live. And yet, you run from God in disobedience to His call. You submerge yourself in your work. You make excuses why you can't serve God on a consistent basis. You justify your un-involvement in the lives of others while pursuing the desires of your heart; but never without consequence.

The prophet Jonah had to deal with the consequence of his disobedience to God, and so it is with us all. When you know the will of God and choose to run from it, there is a price to pay. Why? Because you cannot successfully run from God, no matter how hard you try. Jonah was unsuccessful in running from God. When God commissioned Jonah to go to Nineveh to preach a message of condemnation for their wickedness, Jonah defiantly disobeyed. The disobedience of the prophet led to a consequence. Though Jonah ran in the opposite direction of Nineveh, he was not successful in escaping from the sovereign hand of God. God sent a storm and a giant fish to set Jonah back on the right track. And After three days and three nights in the belly of the fish, the Bible says, (this time) "Jonah obeyed, and sent to Nineveh" (Jonah 3:3).

What type of storm has God placed in your life to set your back on the right track? What type of giant fish has God sent to swallow you whole? Some of you know that the direction you're taking is in direct defiance of God's Word and call on your life. You cannot successfully run from God. When you do, there are consequences to pay. Therefore, stop running from God. Stop trying to live life in your own strength and your own ability without the leading and direction of Almighty God. You cannot fight Satan in your own strength. He'll beat you every time. Nor can you hold your personal or professional life together apart from God. That's why you must see that God has a plan for your life that includes Him and other brothers and sisters in Christ who can help you and encourage you to be the kind of person that He intends for you to be. Many people are running from God and they go to church every Sunday. Others make cameo appearances in church pretending that everything is alright when in reality all hell has broken loose in their personal lives but they're too proud or too ashamed to admit it.

As a result of the consequences of disobedience, when you hear the Word of God, do like Jonah; (this time) obey His will and keep His commandments knowing that as a Christian, you are here to make a heavenly impact in a wicked society that God has commissioned you to go in, to live in, and to proclaim His Word in. Starting today, obey God's will for your life.

You Can't Be A Real Success Without God

"...I decided that there was nothing better for a man to do than to enjoy his (or her) food and drink, and his (or her) job. Then I realized that even this pleasure is from the hand of God. For who can eat or enjoy apart from Him? For God gives those who please Him wisdom, knowledge, and joy" (Ecclesiastes 2:24b-26a, TLB)

Solomon, the author of Ecclesiastes, King of Israel, lived a long life. He had wealth, opulent homes, servants, power, prestige, education, beautiful women at his every beckoning call, and yet he said, "I looked at everything I had tried, it was all so useless, a chasing of the wind, and there was nothing really worthwhile anywhere" (Ecclesiastes 2:11, TLB). Materially, Solomon had it all, but he was still left with an empty feeling deep down inside. Though he appeared to have everything, he knew he had nothing. Though people saw him as a success, he knew he was a failure without Almighty God. Solomon said, "everything is unutterably weary and tiresome (apart from God). No matter how much we see, we are never satisfied; not matter how much we hear, we are not content (apart from God)" (Ecclesiastes 1:8). And we today are no different.

Apart from the God there can be no real success in your life, only things that satisfy temporarily. Satisfaction and contentment can only be maintained in your life as you nurture and develop a close relationship with God through Christ. God is the true measure of your earthly success. Why? Because, "pleasure (and success) is from the hand of God...for God gives those who please Him wisdom, knowledge, and joy." No job, relationship, education, wealth, or material possession will ever give you the real success that can only be found in God through Jesus Christ our Lord. Therefore, true success can be summarized this way: "fear God (through Christ) and obey His commandments, for this is the entire duty of man" (Ecclesiastes 12:13).

Make God the number one priority of your life, and you will be successful. Your relationship with God through Christ is the true measure of real success. I encourage you today to succeed.

You Can't Grow If You Don't Know!

"Study to show thyself approved unto God, a workman that needeth not to be ashamed, rightly dividing the word of truth" (2 Timothy 2:15)

How many books, gospels, and epistles (letters) make up the Bible? What is the central theme of the Bible? What does the Bible say about salvation? What does the Bible say about your relationship with God through Jesus Christ? What is the Holy Spirits role in your life? What does the Bible say about faith in your everyday life? These are basic questions thousands of churchgoers across the country and world cannot answer because they haven't taken the time to study the Bible for themselves resulting in baby Christians afraid to share their faith because they don't really know what they believe concerning Jesus Christ. And so, you have people who attend church every Sunday, year in and year out unable to "rightly divide the word of truth." Why? Because they haven't studied the Word to show themselves approved of God as workmen that need not be ashamed of the gospel of Jesus Christ.

You can't grow in your Christian life if you don't take the time to know God and His Word. The Bible is clear on how husbands and wives should treat each other, how parents are to treat their children and how children should act toward their parents. The Bible clearly points out how we should work in the workplace, how we should spend our money and time during the course of life as we surrender our lives and dreams to Almighty God. But you can't grow in your faith if you don't know about your faith. Therefore, begin studying the Bible for yourself. Invest in a good study Bible with notes at the bottom of the pages. You may even want to buy a good commentary to assist you in rightly dividing the Word. Get into a sound Bible study group and church that can help you in your spiritual growth, and watch what happens. To your surprise, you will grow!

And if you happen to be a teacher of the spiritually uninformed, "Be humble when you are trying to teach those who are mixed up concerning the truth. For if you talk meekly and courteously to them they are more likely, with Gods help, to turn away from their wrong ideas and believe what is true. Then they will come to their senses and escape from Satan's trap of slavery to sin" (2 Timothy 2:25, 26a TLB).

Everyone who names the name of Christ has the capacity to grow in their Christian faith by diligently seeking God through prayer and the diligent study of His Word. You can grow in what God's Word says and what it means by diligently studying His Word to show yourself approved. You can grow as you begin to know.

You Don't Have To Live A Hellish Life!

"Pride goes before destruction, a haughty spirit before a fall" (Proverbs 16:18)

The key to spiritual prosperity in any person's life is humility and obedience to God sound biblical doctrine. Your life must be controlled by God through faith in His Word. But faith in God in not faith if it is not accompanied by humility and obedience.

The Bible says, "For there are six things and Lord hates—no, seven: haughtiness (arrogance & pride), lying, murdering, plotting evil, eagerness to do wrong, a false witness, sowing discord among brothers" (Proverbs 6:16-19). And yet everyday, thousands of people who profess Christianity refuse to humble themselves to the will of God which is the Word of God, instead to practice the things God hates; and they wonder why their lives are so hellish.

I have given biblical counsel to single and married people alike, and many have refused to apply it leading to broken hearts, broken relationships, unwanted pregnancies, unequally yoked marriages, rebellious children, estranged relatives, and even mental breakdowns resulting in a hellish life and a hellish situation. All because "Pride goes before destruction" and "a haughty (arrogant) spirit before a fall" (Proverbs 16:18).

You cannot willfully disobey God and expect peace and joy in your life. It's not going to happen. When you say in your heart, "I know what the Bible says, BUT…" you have just sinned before God because you have chosen not to humble yourself before God, and God hates that. You basically say at that point. "God I don't believe you're asking me to forgive that person or to love that person or to submit to that person, when if fact that's exactly what God is telling you to do. Such biblical actions lead to peace and joy because you're choosing to commit yourself and those in your life to God, by faith in Him.

Many people are living hellish lives solely because they won't let go of their pride, their anger, their arrogance, their sinful habits and hidden secrets, or their wicked schemas; all things they may have grown up with or around, but all things that will eventually lead to destruction and failure in their lives. Now that you know the Word of God concerning your life, your relationships, and even your future, you have not one to blame but yourself if you allow pride and a haughty (arrogant) spirit to dominate your life.

Therefore, don't let pride and a haughty spirit destroy your marriage, your single life, your career, your social life, your future life. Don't be so stubborn to lose everything that is dear to you. Humble yourself before God through His Word by faith in obedience to what it says. You don't have to live a hellish life. By faith in God, your life can be heavenly.

You Have A Purpose For Living!

Jesus said, "All authority in heaven and one earth has been given to me. Therefore go and make disciples of all nations, baptizing them in the name of the Father and of the Son and of the Holy Spirit, and teaching them to obey everything I have commanded you. And surely I am with you always, to the very end of the age" (Matthew 28:1820)

After Christ's resurrection from the dead, the Bible says, "Mary Magdalene, Mary and mother of James, and Salome bought spices so that they might go to anoint Jesus' body" (Mark 16:1). Of course He wasn't there. But the women were told by "a young man dressed in a white robe" (an angel)" (Mark 16:5) to "go, tell His disciples and Peter, 'He is going ahead of you into Galilee. There you will see Him, just as He told you" (Mark 16:7). They didn't believe the angel. This is how the women responded: "Trembling and bewildered, the women went out and fled from the tomb" (Mark 16:8a), and guess what? "They said nothing to anyone, because they were afraid (Mark 16:8b). Jesus eventually appeared to Mary Magdalene who was more interested in who stole His body that His resurrection, said to Jesus Himself, "Sir, if you carried him (Jesus) away, tell me where you have put Him" (John 20:15). The Bible says that, "afterward Jesus appeared in a different form to two of them (His disciples) while they were walking in the country. These returned and reported it to the rest (of the disciples); but they did not believe them either" (Mark 16:12,13). "Later Jesus appeared to the Eleven (disciples) as they were eating" (Mark 16:14a). Guess what He had to do? "He rebuked them for their lack of faith and their stubborn refusal to believe those who had seen Him after He had risen" (Mark 16:14). After Christ's death they had no purpose for living other than to survive. They depended more on the natural than the supernatural power of God. As a result, each disciple involved in experiencing Christ's resurrection responded with a lack of faith. They responded with trembling, bewilderment, fear, and disbelief because to them the problem they were facing with the loss of

Christ appeared larger than the purpose for which they were called to execute: "Go and make disciples of nations" (Matthew 28:19).

Jesus Christ, the Son of the living God gave His disciples a purpose and a reason for living. Their goal was to impact their world in such a way that lives would be changed forever through faith in Him alone! People who had sought happiness and satisfaction through fame and notoriety, money and materialism, position and influence, relationships and immorality were to be taught by Christ' disciples to obey everything He had commanded them knowing that He will always be with them to the very end of the age. And so, once Christ's disciples had a purpose for living, there was no problem too great for them to face. No trial they couldn't handle. No setback that could not be overcome. No dilemma that could not be handled through faith in Christ. Why? Because when you become a purpose driven Christian who depends on the supernatural power of Jesus Christ, there is no trembling, bewilderment, fear, or disbelief that you cannot handle knowing that Christ is always there with you working on your behalf in the power of the Holy Spirit.

We as Christians must always understand that we have a purpose for being here. We have answers to this worlds problems that can only be solved through the good news of Jesus Christ, and God has given us the privilege of being His ambassadors to spread that message of hope to the world in which we live. Therefore, know that as a representative of the kingdom of God, you have a purpose for living and that purpose always starts with Christ. Whatever your background, whatever your lot in life, make Christ you number one reason for living. And rest assured, He is with you always, to the very end of the age.

You Have To Decide To Live By Faith!

"Now the just shall live by faith; But is anyone draws back, (God says) my soul has no pleasure in him (or her)" (Hebrew 10:38)

Receiving Jesus Christ as your savior is not the end but the beginning of your faith. It is upon receiving Jesus Christ that you begin to live by faith in the Holy Word of God, the Bible. It is a process that begins when you decide to live your life based on biblical principles. And so, you have to decide to live by faith in order to find favor with your adopted Father who art in heaven. The Bible says, without faith it is impossible to please God, because anyone who comes to Him must believe that He exists and that He rewards those who earnestly seek Him" (Hebrews 11:6). God rewards those who earnestly seek Him by faith, but you have to make the decision to actually live by faith instead of by what you think and how you feel.

The prophet Habakkuk first wrote the words, "Behold the proud, his soul is not upright in him; but the just shall live by faith" (Habakkuk 2:4). Those that live by faith live by the instructions of God found in His Word. Those who make the decision to live based on how they feel and think about a particular situation apart from the Bible are considered proud in the sight of God and His soul has no pleasure in their decisions.

Anyone who "draws back" from faith in God make the biggest mistake possible. Why? Because, your emotional instincts and feelings will let you down if you have not decided to live by faith in God through Christ. That's why King Solomon wrote, "Trust in the Lord with all your heart and lean not on your own understanding; in all your ways acknowledge Him and He will make your paths straight""(Proverbs 3:5,6). When you decide to live by faith in Christ, God will make your paths straight. He'll straighten out your life, your perspective on life, your relationships in life, your hopes and dreams concerning life, rewarding you with spiritual fullness within your life. And it all starts when you decide to live by faith in God through Christ. But it's your decision to live by faith. Either you will continue to lean on your own understanding and suffer the negative con sequences of your actions, or you will decide to "trust in the Lord with all your heart acknowledging God in all you ways" which will allow you to reap the benefits of God straightening out your life. Either way, you have to make the decision. But if you want God to straighten out your life and reward you as you earnestly seek Him then you have to decide to live by faith in Him. "The just shall live by faith" (Hebrews 10:38).

You Have To Deny Yourself To Win!

"To win the contest you must deny yourselves many things that would keep you from doing your best. An athlete goes to all this trouble just to win a blue ribbon or a silver cup, but we do it for a heavenly reward that never disappears" (1 Corinthians 9:25 TLB)

Thousands of people begin their Christian lives out with a positive bang. They receive Jesus Christ as their Lord and Savior. They tell others about the free gift of eternal life available through Christ. They actively serve in their local church. They read their Bible; give of their time and money, pray on a consistent basis. But along the way, they run out of gas. They lose their focus, purpose, and drive to live for God through Christ as a result of the distractions each person is promised to face in life. They stop reading their Bible, they stop attending church on a weekly basis, and they stop serving God as their Lord and Savior, all because they lost sight of what they were here to compete for.

Paul says, concerning our lifelong competition to serve God, "you must deny yourselves many things that would keep you from doing your best" (1 Corinthians 9:25). What is keeping you from doing your best for God? Hebrews 12:1 reads, "let us strip off anything that slows us down or holds us back, and especially those sins that wrap themselves so tightly around our feet and trip us up; and let us run with patience the particular race that God has set before us." You have to deny yourself sin to win at living for Christ. It's not an easy task but each Christian possesses the power to do so through the Holy Spirit. The Bible says, "Keep your eyes on Jesus, our leader and instructor" (Hebrews 12:2a). Our reward is a "heavenly reward that never disappears." A reward that we can obtain as we train ourselves through God's Word to live right before Him.

Let us not compromise on our Christian faith. Commit your life to living for Christ denying yourself those things that are not pleasing to Him. Keep your eyes on Jesus, our leader and instructor striving to do your best by faith in God through Christ. And without question, you will win a heavenly reward that never disappears. Praise God for denial! Praise God for the reward that awaits you in heaven at the finish line!

You Have To Make Time!

"I have hidden your word in my heart that I might not sin against you". (Psalm 119:11)

During times of stress, pressure, and doubt, people have the tendency to return to those things that soothe them or deaden their pain. Some people return to alcohol, drugs, gambling, pornography, illicit sex, food, shopping, while others return to anger, gossip, maliciousness, excessive work, the psychic hotline, and the like, all in an attempt to ease the stress, pressure, and doubt of their fast paced lives.

As a result of our natural tendencies to satisfy flesh more than satisfying God, we must make the time each day, to soothe ourselves with the Word of God. The Psalmist who was persecuted by men who sought to discredit him and put him to shame writes, "I seek you (Lord) with all my heart; do not let me stray from your commands" (Psalm 119:10). "I have hidden your word in my heart that I might not sin against you" (Psalm 119:11). The Psalmist protected himself from the outside distractions and pressures by soothing himself with the Word of God so that he might not sin against God. He knew that God's Word was the only thing that could sufficiently fill his empty soul. So he made the time to follow the precepts of God. He would further write, "This has been my practice: I obey your precepts" (Psalm 119:56). "Turn my heart toward your statutes and not toward selfish gain" (Psalm 119:36).

You have to make the time to read and meditate on God's Word so that when the pressures of life come your way, your bruised spirit will be soothed and comforted by it, so that you might not sin against Him. Make the time to read and meditate on God's Word. It is the spiritual food for your soul.

You Now Have The Power To Choose!

"We naturally love to do evil things that are just the opposite from the things that the Holy Spirit tell us to do; and the good things we want to do when the Spirit has His way with us are just the opposite of our nature desires (to sin). These two forces within us are constantly fighting each other to win control over us, and our wishes are never free from their pressures. When you are guided by the Holy Spirit you need no longer force yourself to obey Jewish laws" (Galatians 5:17, 18 TLB)

Let's face it. Sin is pleasurable. It gratifies the flesh while grieving and displeasing God. However, God has called His adopted children to a holy lifestyle. A lifestyle that is impossible to live if we're not depending and leaning on the Holy Spirit." Why? Because we naturally gravitate towards sin.

The Bible says that "we naturally love to do evil things that are just the opposite from the things that the Holy Spirit tells us to do; and the good things we want to do when the Spirit has His way with us are just the opposite of our natural desires (to sin)" (Galatians 5:17 TLB). What I'm saying is that it is natural for us to want to sin, but with the power of the Holy Spirit now residing in us, we now have the power to choose right from wrong. As non-believers of Christ, we didn't have that choice. We used to be slaves to sin because we were slaves of Satan, but not any more. When you sin now as a child of God, you sin because you choose to, not because you have to.

As long as you live in your sinful flesh, you will always have a struggle with sin with "the acts of the sinful nature" being "sexual immorality, impurity and debauchery; idolatry and witchcraft; hatred, discord, jealousy, fits of rage, selfish ambition, dissension, faction and envy; drunkenness, orgies, and the life" (Galatians 5:19-21a). With the Holy Spirit indwelling your life, you now have the power to choose righteousness instead of unrighteousness. The Bible says, "These two forces (righteousness and evil) within us are constantly fighting each other to win control over us, and our wishes are never free from their pressures" (Galatians 5:17 TLB). However, "When you are guided by the Holy

Spirit you need no longer force yourself to obey Jewish laws" (Galatians 5:18). Why? Because the Holy Spirit will guide you to live right anyway. The Holy Spirit empowers you to say no to sin and yes to righteousness. You no longer have any excuses when you fall into sin. When you sin now, you sin because you want to, not because you have to.

So is it a sin to have sinful desires? No! Because you are still a sinner. Your flesh will always have sinful desires, but now you're a sinner saved by grace through Jesus Christ our Lord with the power of the Holy Spirit residing in you arming you with the strength to say no to those sinful desires. You're always going to have to struggle with sinful desires but you now have the power to say no to them. And as you humble yourself to be guided by the Holy Spirit your desires begin to line up with the righteous desires of Almighty God.

You no longer have to be a slave to your past or present sins because you have the Holy Spirit working in you seeking to control your life so that your life produces "love, joy, peace, patience, kindness, goodness, faithfulness, gentleness and self-control" (Galatians 5:22, 23). Therefore, let go of the sin that hinders your walk with God and make the decision to follow God through the guiding of His Spirit. The choice is yours. You now have the power to choose righteousness over unrighteousness.

You've Been Set Free, Indeed!

"If the Son (of God) sets you free, you will be free indeed" (John 8:36)

Why do so many people who know the truth of God find themselves still enslaved to sin? Because the sinner cannot break free from sin by his or her own strength when flirting with a sinful environment. People place themselves in situations and environments that breed sin, and then they wonder why they weren't strong enough to overcome the sin. And yet, we make countless resolutions each year, with good intentions surrounding ourselves with temptations that our bodies don't have the strength to defeat. As a result, we will ultimately break our resolutions because we're not physically strong enough to break the shackles of sin when waltzing with the sin that we're trying to break from.

Jesus said, "if the Son sets you free, you will be free indeed" (John 8:36). Jesus being the true seed of Abraham (see Galatians 3:16) can help you break free from the enticements of sin, if you really want to break free from the sin. The Apostle Paul puts it this way: "I put this in human terms because you are weak in your natural selves. Just as you used to offer the parts of your body in slavery to impurity and to ever-increasing wickedness, so now offer them in slavery to righteousness leading to holiness" (Romans 6:19)

Here's how we're to break the cycle of sin in our lives: 1) Flee from those sinful persons, places, or things where you use "to offer the parts of your body in slavery to impurity." Stay away from things that the parts of your body are weak to. 2) Now, offer the parts of your body to God through Christ in prayer, bible study, Sunday morning worship, fellowship and fun times with other believers in Christ, and to the work of the ministry at your local assembly. "Offer them (the parts of your body) in slavery to righteousness leading to holiness" (Romans 6:19)

Stop trying to conquer your sinful habits by yourself in your own strength in a sinful environment you're destined to fail in. Apart from Christ, you won't be able to do it. But with Christ, as you fix your eyes on Him and as you learn to stay clear of those people and those places and those things that you cannot handle in your own strength, and as you replace your sinful environment with a righteous one, you will be set free from sin, indeed.

You Want To Be In The Book Of Life

"An I saw the dead, great and small, standing before the throne (of Christ), and books were opened. Another book was opened, which is the book of life. The dead were judged according to what they had done as recorded in the books"..."If anyone's name was not found written in the book of life, he (or she) was thrown into the lake of fire" (Revelation 20:12,15)

Some people are on counting on their works to get them into heaven, but the Bible says, "all our righteous acts (in the sight of God) are like filthy (menstrual) rags" (Isaiah 64:6b). Some people believe that God is going to weigh their good against their bad, which will enable them to eventually get into heaven. But the Bible says, "the wages (or payment) of (your) sin is death" (Romans 6:23). In other words, your good works are not good enough to get you to heaven. So in the end, you want your name in the book of life not inn the books.

The Bible speaks of two judgments; one for believers known as the bema seat judgment to see what rewards they will receive in heaven after accepting the free gift of eternal life through Jesus Christ. The other judgment will be for people who chose not to receive Jesus as their savior but rather preferred to rely on their good works and good deeds to get them to heaven known as the great white throne judgment.

At the end of this world as we now know it, at the great white throne judgment, the Bible reads, "Then I saw a great white throne and Him who seated on it (Jesus Christ). Earth and sky fled from His presence, and there was no place for them. And I saw the dead (nonbelievers), great and small, standing before the throne, and books (plural) were opened. Another book was opened (singular), which is the book of life (those that received Jesus as Lord and Saviors were in it)" (Revelation 20:11,12). And guess what? The dead, those who chose to work their way to heaven, were judged according to what they had done as recorded in the books (plural)" (Revelation 20:12b). And you know what's going to happen to those nonbelievers who rejected Christ' invitation of eternal life through Him? The Bible says, "Then death and Hades (or Hell) were thrown into the lake of fire. The lake of fire is the second death" (unsaved with these words: "If anyone's name was not found written in the book of life (made possible through Christ), he was thrown into the lake of fire" (Revelation 20:15).

You want to be in the book of life. That is only made possible through acknowledging that you cannot save yourself, because you can't, and by accepting God's free gift of eternal life through Christ. Your works cannot save you, and if you think that, you're in for a tragic surprise. At the great white throne judgment, the only ones who will escape the lake of fire are those whose names are written in the book of life. You don't want your name written in the books. Avoid this judgment by receiving Jesus Christ as your Lord and Savior. Believe me, you'll want your name written in the book of life. God Bless you all.

You've Been Called To A Higher Standard!

"Obey God because you are His children; don't slip back into your old ways—ding evil because you knew no better. But be holy now in everything you do just as the Lord is holy, who invited you to be His child" (1 Peter 1:14, 15 TLB)

Growing up, I was identified as Charlie's boy. I was expected to carry the family name with pride and honor wherever I went. My actions were to reflect my upbringing and the identification with my family who raised me. I was taught to know the difference between right and wrong, and though my family loved me, I was justly punished when I chose to do the latter. Well the same is true of men and women who are now identified with Christ and who have been adopted into the family of God.

As children of God, our heavenly Father expects us to live a righteous life, and He's in-dwelt us with His Spirit, the Holy Spirit, to enable us to "be holy now in everything we do just as the Lord is holy." Before Christ, we lived our lives based on old habits and ways that satisfied our flesh but didn't necessarily satisfy God because we didn't know any better. But now that we've received Christ as our Lord and Savior not only do we know better, but we have the power through the Holy Spirit to obey God. We have been called to a higher standard of living. Now that we are God's adopted children through Jesus Christ, as Paul has stated, "we can do all things through Him who strengthens us" (Philippians 4:13). The question is, are you willing to let go of that old sinful lifestyle even though you know better? God says you can be holy, for He is holy. He's given you the power to shed your sinful past and to move forward into a righteous future.

Well how do you start? First, take it to the Lord in prayer. Secondly, listen to God through His Word. Thirdly, speak honestly to God about your sinful weaknesses and surrender them to Him knowing that "when the Holy Spirit controls our lives He will produce...in us: love, joy peace, patience, kindness, goodness, faithfulness, gentleness and self-control (Galatians 5:22, 23a); the higher standard that God has called us to.

It's time to obey God because you are now identified with Him through Christ. Carry yourself with pride and honor knowing that you are a child of a holy God who invited you to be His child and to walk in holiness for which you have been called.

EPILOGUE

This book is great to use individually or with a group of women who you may know that are tired of ending up with the wrong guy over and over again. Stop the cycle of self abuse and self disrespect at the hands of Mr. Wrong, and use this book to your advantage in taking emotional and spiritual control of your life. Mr. Right will be drawn to the new you while you'll be able to spot Mr. Wrong a mile a way.

For daily inspiration, pick up my 488 page inspirational book, *Powerful Words to Live By: Inspiration for the Soul* to give you that daily spiritual boost to get you on your way. These resources can be purchased at **www.1stbooks.com** or ordered through any Barnes and Noble bookstore. You can also pick up a copy through Amazon.com.

For the best results in using this small yet powerful book, please make sure to answer the questions at the end of each chapter to help you take full advantage in thinking through who God intends for you to be in spite of the past you may have come from. You now have in your hands a book that will help you see yourself in a positive way as you seek to break the negative cycle of unhealthy relationships and an unhealthy life.

And if this book has also wet your appetite concerning spiritual things regarding God, and faith in God through Jesus Christ His Son, feel free to read Romans 10:9-13 and Ephesians 2:8-10 in the New Testament of the Bible. It's sure to aid you in your search for spiritual enlightenment in heavenly things. And feel free to attend a sound church in your area.

ABOUT THE AUTHOR

Bernard H. Hamilton has devoted his life to inspiring people to be the best they can possibly be from a biblical perspective: spiritually, personally, and professionally. He has spent almost two decades in the pastoral ministry assisting people in their pursuit of right living and personal contentment.

With several years of biblical counseling experience as a Senior Pastor, Bernard has helped people work through troubled times in their marriages, single life, career life, and financial life in helping individuals take control of the destinies God has placed them here on earth to accomplish.

Hamilton's own passion is to inspire the souls of people far and wide in becoming all that God has created them to be so they themselves can be equipped in touching others around them in a positive and biblical fashion. For years he has given of his time, money, and effort in helping others reach their spiritual and emotional goals for the betterment of their community and society as a whole.

Bernard lives in Richardson, Texas with his wife, Kimberly and his two daughters, Taylor and Lauren

Bernard H. Hamilton is available for speaking engagements as well as biblical counseling through:

Bernard Hamilton Ministries at **BernardH403@attbi.com** or feel free to call at (972) 480-8721.

0-595-22849-6